Praise for *Ho*

"Fr. Looney's passionate devotion to the Blessed Virgin Mary is both a model and an inspiration for clergy, religious, and anyone who aspires to be a disciple of Jesus Christ. This book will be an impetus for readers to turn to Mary and deepen their appreciation of her, for it echoes in a resounding way the words of Jesus on the Cross to the disciple whom He loved: "Behold your mother." As a bishop, I am convinced that this book will be a lasting resource in the life and ministry of priests, deacons, and seminarians. What a generous and fitting contribution to the life of the Church!"

—Most Reverend David Bonnar, Bishop of Youngstown

"It was while reading these precious lessons from a holy swath of Marian paragons that a thought came: I cannot imagine a more needed book for these times. By introducing our Heavenly Mother in such a fashion, Fr. Edward Looney's words spread a warm wave of maternal protection, efficacy, and direction for readers. As Fr. Donald Calloway has carved out a path as the "St. Joseph priest," Fr. Looney's *How They Love Mary* makes him, in my mind, our "Marian priest." Our world needs mothering now, and Fr. Looney has dug up the holy graves of saints, mystics, Church Doctors, and religious to bring us practical aid from the Queen of all mothers. This book will not leave you unchanged."

—Kevin Wells, author of *The Priests We Need to Save the Church*

"In his usual engaging style, Fr. Looney weaves careful research and personal anecdotes together into beautiful biographical portraits that are at once both broad and deep. I was pleasantly surprised to discover that St. Kateri Tekakwitha, one of my patrons, has a chapter dedicated to her in these pages. I didn't realize until I read this book that she had a devotion to the Blessed Virgin Mary. These pages are simple, accessible, and easy to read, but best savored slowly to appreciate their richness. You, too, will find some pleasant surprises in them."

— Fr. Joel Sember, author of *Oriens:*
A Pilgrimage through Advent and Christmas

"*How They Love Mary* is a master class in embracing Our Lady in a way never presented before this book. Finally there is one text that captures devotions, prayers, examples, saints, lessons, reflections, instructions, stories, inspiration, and references all centered on the Holy Mother of God. What Fr. Edward Looney has assembled is extraordinary. He has found a way to educate us all in a manner that leaves the reader empowered to engage in a deeper understanding of Mother Mary. Fr. Looney invites his readers into a relationship with Mary through the lessons of those who have come before us. Not only does he inform; he also takes the time to supply his reader with the *how*. Reading this book is currently the most complete experience in encountering the Blessed Mother."

— Liv Harrison, talk-show host and podcaster

"This is a very inspiring book, certain to help you grow in love for our Mother. Journey with Fr. Looney through twenty-eight profiles of saints, blesseds, and men and women of faith, and see how they love Mary and how their examples can inspire and challenge us. You will be exposed to many books, devotions, and spiritual practices. A wonderful volume, well worth picking up!"

— Steven R. McEvoy, reviewer at Book Reviews and More

"In Fr. Edward Looney's *How They Love Mary*, we can learn a good deal about the saints and holy people he presents and about the variety of forms Marian devotion has taken on. The book also contains lessons for developing Marian devotion and spirituality. Fr. Looney includes his own experience in this pilgrimage into deeper devotion to Mary—a journey that every reader should take!"

—Rt. Rev. Benedict Neenan, OSB,
Abbot of Conception Abbey, Conception, Missouri

Archbishop Fulton J. Sheen said, "Mary is the woman we all love" As a Marian theologian, Fr. Edward Looney has a great love for the Mother of God that shines forth in the pages of *How They Love Mary*. His treasury of stories offers the reader a myriad of advice on how we, like Fulton Sheen and others, can love Mary in a more meaningful way.

—Al Smith, writer, radio host, and
founder of Bishop Sheen Today

How They Love Mary

Fr. Edward Looney

How They Love Mary
28 Life-Changing Stories
of Devotion to Our Lady

SOPHIA INSTITUTE PRESS
Manchester, New Hampshire

Sophia Institute Press
Box 5284, Manchester, NH 03108
1-800-888-9344
www.SophiaInstitute.com

Sophia Institute Press is a registered trademark of Sophia Institute.

paperback ISBN 978-1-64413-580-8

ebook ISBN 978-1-64413-581-5

Library of Congress Control Number: 2022930839

First printing

Many people have witnessed their love of Mary to me throughout my life: my grandma being the first among them; the ladies from my home parish at Holy Trinity Parish in Oconto who prayed the Rosary after Mass; Joyce Lightner, who led pilgrimages and allowed me to go on a pilgrimage to a Marian apparition site when I was only sixteen years old; fellow seminarians who modeled devotion to Mary and whom I joined in prayer; my mentors in the Mariological Society, especially Fr. James Phalan, CSC, Fr. James Presta, Fr. Fred Miller, and Monsignor Charles Mangan; my parishioners who exhibit a love for the Blessed Mother and whose love I've been able to mold by my preaching and witness; and the unknown pilgrims whom I have observed from afar while visiting Marian shrines throughout the world and whose love for Mary has inspired me. It is to all who have formed my love of Mary, that I dedicate this book.

Contents

Appendices

Introduction

I love Mary! And I know lots of people in the Catholic Church who love Mary. I've met them in parishes, at conferences and on pilgrimages. And the reason we love Mary is because she is our mother and Jesus wants us to love her. Whenever I am asked to give a defense of Marian devotion, I always give the same answer: Jesus loved Mary. St. Paul tells us to be imitators of Christ, and if we wish to fully imitate Jesus, love for His mother must be included. The love that Jesus, the second Person of the Blessed Trinity, had for His Mother can never be outdone by you and me, for we are mere humans, and He was God. We can never love Mary too much because the truth is that Jesus loved her more.

How I, Fr. Edward Looney, Love Mary

I do a lot of speaking engagements, and typically after any given talk someone will ask me: "When did you foster such a love for the Mother of God?" I like to joke and say, "I came out of the womb loving Mary." While I answer in that way to evoke laughter, the answer is not far from the truth. I come from a broken family. My mother and father separated before I was born. My mom lived with my grandma and worked two jobs. She was away from the house a lot. In return, my grandmother became my principal caregiver, and she was a woman devoted to the Blessed Virgin Mary. I have many memories of her holding the rosary and thumbing her beads, quietly sitting in the living room of our house, or with Mother Angelica on EWTN.

During my elementary and middle school years, she often took me to daily Mass, and afterward a group of women would pray the Rosary. I joined them in that prayer. That was the beginning of my love for Mary. A lady from my hometown also organized pilgrimages to a place of purported Marian apparitions. She attended daily Mass, prayed the Rosary, and would share the stories of Mary's many apparitions. Those stories mesmerized me. My curious mind wanted to learn everything about Marian apparitions. This led me to watch *The Song of Bernadette*, starring Jennifer Jones. That film became a bulwark on which my faith was built. The stories of Mary's apparitions became proof to me that God was real, He existed, and that I should try to live the message of the gospel, because, after all, this was the precise reason Mary was appearing on Earth.

When I was sixteen years old, I had the opportunity to go to Europe and visit a few Marian shrines and places of prayer. I was struck by the expressions of a lived faith—people who filled the churches for daily Mass, lined up for Confession, and prayed the Rosary in large numbers. This was not my experience of Catholicism in the small city of four thousand where I grew up. In Europe, I asked myself whether I would ever experience such public witnesses of faith and devotion in my own home area. Little did I know that a few weeks later, on August 15, 2005, I would, at the Shrine of Our Lady of Good Help (now the National Shrine) in Champion, Wisconsin. That day thousands of people gathered for the celebration of an outdoor Mass and Eucharistic procession. Just as at the shrines in Europe, people came out in big numbers to express their love for Mary. This began a new phase of Marian devotion in my life: pilgrimage. In my short life, I have been a pilgrim to many shrines throughout the world—in France, Belgium, Portugal, Ireland, Canada, and the United States. As one person quipped on *Pathways of Learning*, a show on SiriusXM's The Catholic Channel, "When we go to a Marian shrine, it's like we are going home to mom's house." From my experience of pilgrimage, I agree. And I go to mom's house often, whether that's locally at the National Shrine of Our Lady of Good Help, or the National Shrine of Mary, Help of Christians, or a Schoenstatt Chapel, or one of the many shrines of Mary in the United States or abroad. Pilgrimage has been a way I tell Mary I love her and spend time talking to her as my mom.

When I was a junior and senior in high school, I began reading books about Mary. One that sticks out in my mind—I did a book report on it and interviewed the author—was Bud MacFarlane's novel *Pierced by a Sword*. I know there were others, and now, having completed undergraduate and graduate studies, and immersed in the life of academia, I am still reading, especially about Mary. I love learning about her presence in Scripture, her role in history, and her impact on many holy people throughout our tradition. I love Mary through my research, reading, and writing because it's a way I get to know her more and share with others why they ought to love her too. I have recollections from my high school years of meandering to the Mariological Society of America website. Even as an adolescent I had an interest in Marian study, and I wondered if, one day, I might become a Marian scholar. Though I do not possess any formal degree in Mariology, besides focusing my STB research papers on topics of Mariology, I became a member of the society during my college years. And in 2011, I became, to my knowledge, the youngest and most inexperienced person to present at their conference. Apparently, they have received my scholarship favorably, because at present I've presented four academic papers: on the Wisconsin apparition; the Marian thought of Chiara Lubich, foundress of the Focolare movement; the Marian Eucharistic thought of Fr. Daniel Lord, SJ; and the Assumption homilies of Sts. Bernard and Aelred. In 2016, members of the society elected me to one of a handful of positions on their Administrative Council, and in 2020 I was nominated for the office of vice president. This work is yet another way I've identified in my life that I love Mary.

I know that as my life progresses, my love for Mary will only grow, and it will definitely take many forms of expression: devotionally with prayers such as the Rosary, novenas, and litanies (I've written a good number of devotional books), to being clothed with the protection of Mary (especially the brown scapular and the Miraculous Medal), to pilgrimage, and more study. I always ask Mary to help me love Jesus. With all the ways we can love Mary, I hope—like the Ven. Fulton Sheen—that when I meet the Lord face-to-face, He will say, "My mother has told me a lot about you."

Allowing Others to Teach Us How to Love Mary

My academic study of Mary brought me to research the writings of several American figures. In June 2017, while reading on an Amtrak train the biography of another American figure in order to understand how he loved Mary so that I could write an essay for a Catholic publication, and while on pilgrimage to visit the grave of Fr. Daniel Lord, whose Marian thought I had just studied, I recognized the seed of a book germinating in my mind, bringing together past study and inviting me to further study. These figures of American Catholicism taught me new ways of loving Mary that I had not considered previously. Isn't this the role of holy men and women? To inspire to holiness and love of God? This is what the collect for the feast of St. Lawrence of Rome suggests, when we ask God to "help us love what he loved." Another answer I often give to the question of why we should foster a Marian devotion is that it was a way of life for the saints. Think of any of your favorite saints and ask yourself, "Did they have a devotion to Mary?" I'm certain the answer will be yes.

Holy men and women, canonized or not, can become teachers for us in the spiritual life. Sometimes how they lived their life can be an inspiration to us and we can integrate some form of their spirituality into our daily lives. They have something to teach us, and we can learn from them. After all, isn't this the way our education system in the United States works? People more experienced than we are convey the knowledge they have, and as students we learn from them. You can sense how a thinker has influenced the thought of some theologians. The same is true in the spiritual life. For myself, I learn a lot from my peers, and sometimes their own expressions of faith and devotion inspire me to desire holiness to a greater degree. Not only those close to me have this effect, but also those who are more seasoned in the spiritual life.

This book is meant to be a Marian devotional, introducing you to many ways holy men and women have loved Mary throughout time. Some are saints, others are on the way to sainthood, and some should be considered for sainthood. The people featured in this twenty-eight-day devotional are people whose writings I have read and who have touched me in some way. We will hear them speak about Mary and notice different expressions of devotion present in their lives. You might find a new way to love Mary, or you might better appreciate a form of devotion you already practice. There are some saints you would expect me to have selected but I have left out. I have chosen not to include some of them because other authors have done in a similar way what I seek to do with this devotional. For example, *Thirty-Three Days to Morning Glory* by Fr. Michael Gaitley, MIC, explores the Marian thought and devotion of St. Louis de Montfort, St. Maximilian Kolbe, St. Teresa of Calcutta, and St. John Paul II. I don't believe I could have added much to what he wrote, and so I have selected other individuals with whom you might be unfamiliar.

Whether you are a recent convert to the Catholic Faith, and perhaps grew up in a tradition that vehemently opposed any form of Marian devotion, calling it Mariolotry or Mary worship, or have been Catholic all your life, I'm sure this book will have something to offer you. For the newer Catholic seeking to understand Marian devotion, you will discover how others loved Mary and discover some way you can be devoted to her. For your casual, Sunday-going Catholic, maybe Marian devotion was something that never took off in your life or was never taught. As you learn from these witnesses, perhaps you will find a form of loving Mary appropriate for you. For the devout Catholic, perhaps your devotion to Mary has become stagnant and you are looking for something more. I hope the example of these holy people will reignite that fervor.

Do you love Mary like Jesus did? Do you want to love her more, in imitation of Christ? Then you are ready for this journey of deepening that love for the rest of your life.

Lesson 1

Every Saint Is Devoted to Mary in Some Way

St. Damien of Molokai

We all celebrate our birthdays. Some like to ignore them, and others look forward to celebrating with family and friends. The Catholic Church has a liturgical calendar that celebrates the lives of saints. Often these observances commemorate the saint's birth into eternal life (their death date). If that wasn't possible, then some other significant event, such as their conversion or other important date in their life is chosen. If you don't know your birthday saint, you'll want to find out who it is. He may be on the universal calendar or might be an unknown saint celebrated by a local church. For me, born on May 10, my birthday saint is St. Damien of Molokai. I think I first learned this fact from a 365 Saint's Days poster my grandma bought from EWTN's Religious Catalogue. It wasn't until college seminary and beyond that I came to know the story of St. Damien of Molokai and his heroic service as a priest. In 2015, when I visited Belgium to do research, I was sure to visit his tomb in Louvain. When I was ordained a priest, I could include one additional saint in the Litany of Saints; St. Damien was the saint I selected.

St. Damien of Molokai was born in Tremelo, Belgium, on January 3, 1840, and given the name Joseph in honor of the foster father of Jesus. His family had a pious household where prayer and virtue were taught, learned, and lived. Two of his sisters joined religious life and a brother, Pamphile, was also ordained a priest. Pamphile and Damien joined the same religious order, the missionary order called the Congregation of the Sacred Hearts of Jesus and Mary (also called the Picpus Fathers). At the profession of vows, Joseph received the name Damien. The congregation did not believe that Damien had a calling to be a priest because he lacked academic aptitude. It was believed he would remain a brother. He persevered in his studies and was granted the opportunity to study for the priesthood. His service to God's holy people and desire to be a missionary like St. Francis Xavier compelled him to delay his ordination and volunteer to minister in Hawaii in place of his brother, Pamphile. Pamphile was stricken with typhus before he was to leave Belgium, which sidelined him. Damien did not hesitate to go in his place. Once he reached Hawaii, he would need to be ordained by the bishop there in order to begin his priestly ministry and then his lifelong ministry to the leper community in Molokai.

Before he left his beloved country of Belgium, never to return, he was able to visit his family. Together they visited a Marian shrine called Our Lady of Montaigu, a shrine that Damien had walked to as a pilgrim many times. After this visit, he remarked, "I was overcome at thinking that I shall never more see Our Lady of Montaigu. I have asked her to obtain for me from our Lord the grace of laboring in His Vineyard for twelve years."[1] The original shrine of Our Lady of Montaigu was housed in an oak tree, and in the 1600s a church was built on the site. The shrine has been visited

---

[1] Father Pamphile, *Life and Letters of Father Damien: The Apostle of the Lepers* (London: Catholic Truth Society, 1889), 45.

by many saints, including not only St. Damien but also St. John Berchmans. This final visit to Our Lady of Montaigu alongside his family was one St. Damien wanted to treasure in his heart. What a beautiful image to behold: a mother praying for her missionary son and a son praying for his mission and the protection of his family. As Damien set off for Hawaii, aboard ship he continued his Marian devotion by beginning a novena to the Blessed Virgin, which was to end on February 2, then celebrated as the Purification of the Virgin Mary, today known as the Presentation of Jesus in the Temple.

The Marian devotion of St. Damien of Molokai was a simple one. He did not write books or treatises on the Blessed Mother, but he promoted devotion to the scapular and wanted individuals to be enrolled in the confraternity associated with the devotion. As a member of the Congregation of the Sacred Hearts he fostered a devotion to the Sacred Heart of Jesus and the Immaculate Heart of Mary. When he wrote letters to his family, he would sign them: "In Union with the Sacred Hearts of Jesus and Mary" or "In the Sacred Hearts." A simple, small act of Marian devotion, but it communicates to us that he strived to live his life in union with the two hearts. He wanted to love like Jesus and Mary. In one letter to his parents, he told them, "Such are the heartfelt wishes offered up daily on your behalf to the Sacred Hearts of Jesus and Mary."[2] Not only did he live in union with the two hearts, but he offered to the two hearts those he loved and cared about. In another letter, he prayed for his family, saying, "May the Blessed Virgin grant you the grace of a holy death, which will be followed by a happy eternity."[3] The Rosary also had a place in the life of

---

[2] Pamphile, *Life and Letters*, 42.
[3] Pamphile, *Life and Letters*, 50.

St. Damien. In another letter to his family, he asked them to "say your rosary every evening for the missioners."[4]

St. Damien did so much in Molokai. Besides being their priest, he was a quasi-doctor, funeral director, coffin builder, and grave-digger. He buried many people each week. He commented to his brother, "My greatest pleasure is to go there [the garden of the dead] to say my beads and meditate on the unending happiness which so many of them are already enjoying."[5] The Rosary became a tool for him to remember the dead and meditate on the life to come. And as St. Damien would contract leprosy and succumb to it in 1889, he was able to ask Mary to pray for him at the hour of his death.

There is a line of a Marian hymn that says, "Every saint has praised her." This is a lesson that my birthday saint has taught me. He praised her and wanted others to be devoted to her. His devotion was not extravagant. It was enough for him. I wish I could have read some of his homilies or his reflections on Mary, but I know that he honored her like every other saint, and so in simple ways I can love Mary just like he did.

How to Love Mary Like St. Damien of Molokai

• Who is your birthday saint? Look it up online. Maybe add to your search the name of Mary, too. For example, if your birthday saint is St. Philip Neri, search the following: "St. Philip Neri + Blessed Virgin Mary." Maybe you will find a quote or a devotion that he loved.

Pamphile, *Life and Letters*, 49.
5 Pamphile, *Life and Letters*, 118.

- Learn the story of a local Marian shrine in your diocese, state, or neighboring state. Why was it built? Plan to make a pilgrimage and spend some time in prayer there.
- How do you sign your letters or e-mails? Would you ever consider signing them with a religious notation?
- Heed the advice of St. Damien and pray a Rosary today. Begin your Rosary saying something like this: "Dear Blessed Mother, I offer this Rosary today for all those who are missionaries, for those who have left their home country to preach the gospel." We are mindful that many missionary priests serve the United States in our parishes, filling pastoral needs. If you have a missionary priest as your pastor, offer your Rosary for him.
- Visit a cemetery, go for a walk, and pray the Rosary, meditating on the glorious mysteries as you await your journey to Heaven.

Lesson 2

A Greeting for Mary

St. Francis of Assisi

St. Francis of Assisi is one of the most popular saints in Catholicism. Many homes I visit have statues of St. Francis in their gardens or on a patio. He is a loveable saint because of his love for nature, creation, and animals. Our churches sing songs inspired by his life and words as we ask God to make us channels of His peace or sing the glory of creation. People like to quote him as saying, "Preach the gospel at all times; if necessary, use words," though it's doubtful if he ever said these words. Nevertheless, they are true, and they embody the Franciscan spirit.

I can't say that I have had a deep devotion to St. Francis throughout my life, but my affection for St. Francis results from my association at Baptism with him. The pastor of my hometown at the time I was born was a Franciscan friar from the Assumption BVM province in Pulaski, Wisconsin. The priest's name was Fr. Vianney, and I had the opportunity to get to know him in my last years of seminary. The retirement home for his province was just south of Milwaukee, and on my way home from seminary, I would stop and visit him. A few years into my priesthood, Fr. Vianney passed away, and I was blessed to be present and concelebrate at his funeral Mass.

How They Love Mary

The Franciscan order has been known for its Marian devotion and doctrine since its foundation. Blessed Duns Scotus provided the theological framework for the dogma of Mary's Immaculate Conception. Many other Franciscan saints have promoted devotion to Mary, chief among them St. Maximillian Kolbe and St. Lawrence of Brindisi. This book will feature others, including Blessed Solanus Casey and St. Pio of Pietrelcina. The Marian devotion of these saintly men was formed by the Marian heritage of the Franciscan order, beginning with their inspired founder, St. Francis of Assisi.

St. Francis of Assisi, born in 1181 or 1182, was a son of wealthy parents. He felt called to renounce this wealth and become a poor beggar, stripping himself of his garments. His friends sought him out to help him find his way back to a normal life, but they were so convicted by his radical poverty that they followed him and his way of life. After founding the Order of Friars Minor, he and his devoted follower St. Clare founded a female branch of the Franciscan family. Today, those women religious are known as the Second Order of St. Francis of Assisi, or Poor Clares.

We owe much of the modern Christmastide devotion to Mary to St. Francis—namely, the Nativity scene. It came about when St. Francis was visiting the town of Greccio for Christmas. In order to encourage the people to celebrate with greater solemnity, he crafted the first manger scene. Every time we look upon the Holy Family around Christmas, we have St. Francis to thank for lifting our minds and hearts to contemplate that God became man and was born of the Virgin in Bethlehem.

We can go from crib to cross in the life of St. Francis because he had a tremendous devotion to Christ Crucified. In the year 1224, St. Francis received the wounds of Christ in his body, called the *stigmata*, thus bearing witness to the love and suffering of Christ by his very life. It was from a crucifix, known as the San Damiano Cross, that St. Francis heard the voice of Jesus tell him to rebuild His church. And Francis penned the Office of the Passion, which was recited by the friars. One of the antiphons of the Office of the Passion salutes Mary this way: "Holy Virgin Mary, among the women born into the world, there is no one like you. Daughter and servant of the most high and supreme King of the Father in heaven, Mother of our most holy Lord Jesus Christ. Spouse of the Holy Spirit, pray for us." This antiphonal prayer emphasizes the uniqueness of Mary and her relationship to the Trinity as Father, Son, and Spirit. The Office of the Passion serves as a reminder of Christ's death on the Cross and Mary's proximity to Calvary.

Our Lady of the Angels is closely associated with the Franciscan order. The feast is celebrated on August 2 and carries a major indulgence. This devotion stems from St. Francis's work at the Church of Our Lady of Angels—also known as the Portiuncula—in his hometown of Assisi. Many would say that the restoration of the Portiuncula marks the birth of the Franciscan order. According to St. Bonaventure, St. Francis put Mary in charge of the order as its patron and advocate. St. Francis also took up penance, fasting in her honor from the feast of Sts. Peter and Paul to the feast of the Assumption, observing a sort of mini Lent. St. Francis sensed a special presence of angels at the Portiuncula. He drew near to this chapel, dedicated to Our Lady of the Angels, and there allowed his Marian devotion to take form and shape.

St. Francis also wrote about the Blessed Virgin in the form of a prayer to Our Lady. It is called the Salutation to the Blessed Virgin and is considered an authentic writing of St. Francis. The Salutation is a form of greeting to Mary:

Hail O Lady, Holy Queen, Mary, holy
    Mother of God,
Who are the Virgin Made Church,
Chosen by the most Holy Father in Heaven
Whom He consecrated with His most holy
    beloved Son
And with the Holy Spirit the Paraclete,
In whom there was and is all fullness of
    grace and every good.
Hail His Palace!
Hail His Tabernacle!
Hail His Dwelling!
Hail His Robe!
Hail His Servant!
Hail His Mother!
And hail all You holy virtues
Which are poured into the hearts of the
    faithful
Through the grace and enlightenment of
    the Holy Spirit,
That from being unbelievers,
You may make them faithful to God.

This beautiful salutation offers a snapshot into how St. Francis saw the Blessed Virgin. It acknowledges that Mary was chosen by the Father and consecrated for this role in salvation history. Mary is closely associated with the Holy Spirit. He finds reason for us to "Hail Mary" under different symbolic titles. Mary as the palace of God, the tabernacle, the dwelling place of God. God chose to take on flesh and become incarnate through the womb of Mary. For nine months she was all these things, as in her body she contained the living God. "Hail His Servant!" Indeed we do, because Mary called herself a servant of the Lord when she gave her fiat. The salutation greets Mary most especially as mother, for she is the Mother of God, and the mother of all people, for Francis entrusted his confreres to her as sons of this Heavenly Mother.

The Marian devotion of the order St. Francis founded continued long after his death, as noted earlier. A popular devotion to Our Lady came out of the Franciscan tradition called the Franciscan Crown, also known as the Seraphic Rosary. The Franciscan Crown has seven decades focusing on the joys of Mary—the Annunciation, the Visitation, the Nativity of Jesus, the Adoration of the Magi, the Finding in the Temple, the Resurrection of Jesus, and the Assumption and Coronation of Mary. Legend has it that in 1442 a Franciscan novice named James received an apparition of Our Lady in Assisi. This young novice would daily bring a crown of roses to Mary, but after entering the order and following the vow of poverty, he no longer was able to and was grieved by that. Mary appeared and told him that she would like a daily offering of seven decades meditating on her seven joys. The devotion of Friar James was noticed by his brothers and soon began to spread throughout the Franciscan order.

St. Francis greeted the Blessed Virgin Mary in his prayer and through his Salutation. We continue to greet her with his words and by imitating his life. St. Francis was a son of Mary who meditated upon her life, entrusted his order to her intercession, and greeted her in his prayer. Like him, let us address Our Lady with our love and devotion.

How to Love Mary Like St. Francis of Assisi

- Recite the Office of the Passion.
- Pray the Salutation to the Blessed Virgin Mary.
- Pray the Franciscan Crown—just use your rosary beads and add two additional decades.

Lesson 3

Love Our Lady and Make Her Loved

St. Padre Pio

After the Blessed Mother, Padre Pio is most likely one of the very first saints I became familiar with in my childhood. Officially known as St. Pio of Pietrelcina, Padre Pio was a wonder worker of his time who secured healings for individuals and who (like St. Francis) bore the wounds of Jesus crucified in the stigmata. As a priest-confessor, he was able to read souls.

As a young boy, I was mystified by the story of Padre Pio. People all over Europe would flock to San Giovanni Rotondo, where the saintly friar lived in a Franciscan friary. Pilgrims longed to be a part of his Holy Mass or to have him absolve them of their sins. My first memory of Padre Pio was something I saw on EWTN. One day, they featured an item of the month. If you sent a check to the Old Leeds Road address, they would send you the item. That time, it was a little banner, and it hung in the entryway of my family home for years. It featured an image of Padre Pio and the words he was known for: "Pray, Hope, and Don't Worry." A book about Padre Pio was one of the first nonfiction books of a spiritual nature that I read during my teenage years.

Even though I had such a great interest in Padre Pio, when I thought about the priesthood, I never considered becoming a Capuchin like him. When I came to a critical moment in my priestly discernment, I began a novena to Padre Pio. I'm not sure why. You would have thought it would have been St. Thérèse of Lisieux. I recall that I had just received a little *Padre Pio Prayer Book* in the mail, and perhaps that was the reason why I selected him. I had two options before me that I was discerning. In those nine days, I encountered Padre Pio in unimagined ways. I went to a monastery of nuns to pray one afternoon, and in the pew I was sitting in was a booklet with Padre Pio's famous prayer, Stay with Me, Lord. There was a montage of Padre Pio images on the front. I had a meeting with another priest who was going to help me discern my vocation. I had never been to that priest's office before, and when I arrived, a picture of Padre Pio awaited me. I took it as a sign that I was supposed to return home and discern the priesthood in Green Bay. And so I did.

Padre Pio is a saint beloved by so many Catholics. Devotees of his consider themselves his spiritual children. He once said, "I will take my place at the gate to paradise, but I shall not enter until I have seen the last of my spiritual children enter." With the perpetual devotion to him in the Church, he may be waiting until the resurrection of the body. Padre Pio had quotable phrases that he shared with his spiritual children, and some pertained to the Blessed Mother. There is a famous image of Padre Pio kissing a statue of Our Lady of Fatima. In 1951, he became very sick, and this statue of Our Lady was flown from Fatima to his hospital room. He venerated it and experienced an inexplicable healing.

Padre Pio was born in the village of Pietrelcina in May 1887. He fostered a devotion to Mary at a young age. It is said that, beginning in his youth, he received visits from the Blessed Mother throughout his life. At the age of five, he consecrated himself to the Blessed Mother, and he renewed his Marian consecration each month on the First Saturday as a way for him to fulfill the requests Our Lady made at Fatima to the three children. In his prayer of monthly consecration, he consecrated his entire self to the Blessed Mother and promised "to devote myself wholeheartedly to your service, in order to hasten and assure, through the sovereignty of your Immaculate Heart, the coming of the kingdom of the Sacred Heart of your adorable Son, in our own hearts and in the hearts of all, in our country and in all the world, as in heaven, so on earth."

Padre Pio also loved holy images of Mary. When he entered the novitiate for the Capuchins in 1903, he was greeted by a painting of Our Lady of Sorrows. Next to the image was the exhortation to say a Hail Mary as you passed by the picture. Throughout his life he would pause at countless images of Mary and be caught up in the beauty of Mary. The image of Our Lady of Grace in the sanctuary of the Church in San Giovanni Rotondo became another place where he spent countless hours in prayer, meditation, and contemplation. He had images of Mary in his room and had a phrase nearby reminding him of the teaching of St. Bernard that "Mary is the foundation of my hope."

Padre Pio also fostered a devotion to Mary under several titles: Our Lady of Loreto, Our Lady of Lourdes, Our Lady of Fatima, Our Lady Liberatrix, Our Lady of Grace, Our Lady of Sorrows, Our Lady of Pompeii, and Our Lady of the Assumption. He once was asked if he wanted to visit Lourdes, and he responded by saying that he visited Lourdes every night. Padre Pio was known to have the gift of bilocation—that is, to be in two places at the same time—and he visited the Grotto of Lourdes by praying before an image in his room.

How They Love Mary

The closeness of Mary to the Holy Mass is noted by many saints and theologians. As a priest, I often pray a simple prayer before Mass asking Mary to stand by me as I celebrate Mass as she stood by the crucified Christ on Calvary. The Mass represents Calvary to us each time it is celebrated. Christ is offered as the sacrifice and victim; He is the Lamb of God who takes away the sins of the world. Padre Pio also knew the closeness of Mary while celebrating Mass. On March 1, 1961, he had a mystical experience of Mary accompanying him to the altar for the celebration of Mass. On August 15, 1929, when Padre Pio was offering the Mass, he received an apparition of Our Lady with the Child Jesus; they offered him the consoling words: "Be at peace. We are with you. You belong to us and we are yours." A woman asked Padre Pio to inscribe a prayer in the front of her hand missal. When he gave it back, she saw he had written: "If you want to assist at Holy Mass with devotion and fruitfully, keep company with the Sorrowful Virgin at the foot of the Cross on Calvary." Padre Pio had a keen awareness that Mary's participation in the Mass can deepen our own love for the Holy Mass, the Eucharist, and Mary herself.

Padre Pio was devoted to the Rosary. He was never seen without a rosary in his hand. He was asked by his superiors about how many Rosaries he prayed a day. His answer was more than thirty. Many of us find it difficult to pray just one Rosary consisting of five decades. He prayed the Rosary perpetually. Once when he realized he had forgotten his rosary, he asked a fellow friar to go and retrieve his weapon. His recommendation was to always have a rosary in your pocket or nearby you so you could pray it. He tirelessly promoted and recommended the daily recitation of the Rosary as a means by which we experience the help of Mary in our life. Through the Rosary, he was able constantly to meditate on the life of Jesus. When asked what he wanted to leave his spiritual children as an inheritance, he answered, the Rosary. Padre Pio invites us to rediscover the power of this prayer.

Padre Pio died in 1968, leaving behind a legacy of faith and trust in God. He suffered throughout his life as he bore the wounds of Jesus in his body, and he found consolation in his devotion to Our Lady, who suffered alongside Jesus. He once said, "Love the Blessed Mother and make her loved." By his example and teachings, he is making her loved, and now, like him, we seek to love the Blessed Mother in our daily life.

How to Love Mary Like Padre Pio

* Consecration to Mary can be done through a long process of preparation like that proposed by St. Louis de Montfort. Or you can pray a simple prayer of consecration: "My Queen and my Mother, I give myself entirely to you; and to show my devotion to you, I consecrate to you this day my eyes, my ears, my mouth, my heart, my whole being without reserve. Wherefore, good Mother, as I am your own, keep me, guard me, as your property and possession. Amen."
* Sit for a few moments with your favorite image of Mary. It may be hanging in your house; you may pull up a picture on your phone. What goes through your mind as you look into the eyes of Mary? Spend time in quiet prayer.
* Some of Padre Pio's Marian devotions were to local titles of Mary such as Our Lady Liberatrix. Are you aware of any local Marian devotions in your diocese or state?
* The next time you are at Mass, think of how Mary is present at the Mass. As the priest stands at the altar and raises

the Host and chalice, saying "This is my body" and "This is my blood," remember Mary could say those words, as Christ came forth from her womb! She stands there in adoration of the Eucharistic mystery and she stands there as witness to Calvary.

• Padre Pio believed the Rosary was a weapon. It is a way for you to conquer evil in your life. Pray the Rosary today and ask Mary to help you overcome whatever sin you struggle with the most.

Lesson 4

Mary Knows Our Suffering

Mother Angelica

My grandma loved watching EWTN. As a boy, I watched it with her. *St. Michael's Angel Force*, their progamming for youth, was a show I watched in the afternoons. *Life on the Rock* was another show that I would try to watch. I remember it aired live on Thursday nights, and I called in a few times with questions. The same was true for *Sunday Night Live* with Fr. Benedict Groeschel. I always dreamed of someday appearing on EWTN myself. Those dreams have been fulfilled multiple times. Twice I was able to record in person in Irondale, and a few shows were recorded remotely due to the COVID-19 pandemic.

Media has been a passion of mine for a long time. I left college seminary after just one semester and transferred to a college back home. My major was in communications because I wanted to be a journalist, and I enrolled in an introduction to mass communication class. It was an enjoyable class from what I recall. One of our assignments was a research paper, and I chose to write about Mother Angelica as a pioneer in Catholic communications. As I think back to it, I'm pretty sure it was terrible, but it was my first year of college. Nevertheless, I did earn an A in the class.

Needless to say, I wound up in a very different line of work. But my childhood admiration for a nun who sometimes wore an eye patch and who wasn't afraid to be bold in speech propelled me to study her. Many people continue to be impacted by the life and legacy of EWTN as it broadcasts the gospel into their homes and on their smart devices. They still hear her voice as she teaches the faith, shares about her love for Mary, and leads people in the Rosary, along with her nuns, years after her death.

Mother Angelica was born Rita Rizzo in 1923 in Canton, Ohio, to Mae and John Rizzo. While her Baptism was delayed, Rita would be baptized, and afterward her mother brought her to the altar of Our Lady of Sorrows and laid her on the altar, an act indicating a special entrustment to the Virgin Mary.

It was a foreshadowing of what Mother Angelica's future would bring. She knew suffering as a child when she experienced the divorce of her parents. In her adult life, she knew the suffering of illness. In her youth, Mother Angelica fostered a devotion to the Way of the Cross and would bring her sufferings to Our Lady of Sorrows. During her call-in shows, she would offer motherly counsel to individuals facing any number of situations. To one caller, she said, "You have a great cross there, but don't put the cross of bitterness on top of it, because that's when you get hopeless. I want you to take that cross and give it to Mary.... She knows what it means to be abandoned.... Now I'm going to say a prayer for you."[6] In this advice, we see how Mother Angelica dealt with the suffering in her life by turning it over to and uniting it with Mary at the foot of the Cross.

---

[6] Raymond Arroyo, *Mother Angelica: The Remarkable Story of a Nun, Her Nerve, and a Network of Miracles* (New York: Doubleday, 2005), 194.

But first, Rita had to find her own path in life. She discerned she had a vocation and with the help of others she found a religious community to join: the Poor Clares of Perpetual Adoration in Cleveland, Ohio. During her time at this monastery, she oversaw the building of a Marian grotto, which served as a beautiful place for prayer and the fostering of Marian devotion in the community. During her time there, then–Sister Angelica began to feel the prompting of God's call to form a religious community in the south. This led to the foundation of a new community of Poor Clares in Alabama. In the early days of the fledgling community, Mother Angelica found some innovative ways to raise funds for the community and her mission, including the sale of fishing lures. She also began writing and wanted to share these writings with a larger audience, so the nuns began printing her little booklets. Today, many of these early books are published by EWTN Publishing. One in particular addressed the Blessed Virgin Mary and offered keen insights into the different events of Mary's life.

The establishment of EWTN allowed Mother Angelica to broadcast the Rosary and aid people in praying. As a priest, I know many of my homebound parishioners benefit from all the different devotions and programs EWTN has to offer. When I was a young boy, I loved watching the Rosary with Fr. Mitch Pacwa from the different locations in the Holy Land where the Mysteries of the Rosary actually occurred. The afternoon Rosary in my childhood was the International Rosary. I still remember the opening scenes and being mesmerized by all the languages in which the Hail Mary was prayed.

As a cloistered nun, Mother Angelica had a profound devotion to the Rosary. We can encounter Mother Angelica's meditations on the Rosary in *The Prayers and Personal Devotions of Mother Angelica*, compiled and organized by her biographer, Raymond Arroyo.

Mother Angelica recommended praying the Rosary from the heart and suggested one should do all they could to pray three Rosaries a day. She also offered motherly advice on how to pray the Rosary and said that meditation is a must. Here are a few tips she offered:

> When I say the Rosary I allow my soul to gaze at God with great love and admiration; to gaze at the particular mystery. You can take any mystery from the Joyful to the Glorious and admire the perfection of Our Lady or an attribute of God. For instance, look at the Visitation: It's admirable that Our Lady would go to see Elizabeth immediately.[7]

> If you're not making progress in one virtue, say your Rosary and meditate on that virtue as Our Lord practiced it.[8]

> It's all right to get fixed on one mystery. Consider the mystery deeply and pick one aspect of it to meditate upon. For instance, if the mystery is the Annunciation: Our Lady says, 'Be it done to me according to Thy Word.' Well, do I do that?... That's a meditation.[9]

> Forget your mind. Forget your reason. Just admire Our Lady during the Rosary. Admire God for doing the miraculous—the impossible.[10]

This is wisdom from a nun who prayed the Rosary often and who probably struggled at times in her own meditation. But it is wisdom we can incorporate into our own Rosary devotion.

---

[7] Mother Angelica, *The Prayers and Personal Devotions of Mother Angelica* (New York: Doubleday, 2010), 135.
[8] Mother Angelica, *Prayers and Devotions*, 135.
[9] Mother Angelica, *Prayers and Devotions*, 136.
[10] Mother Angelica, *Prayers and Devotions*, 136.

Mother Angelica herself could be considered a mystic because of some of the experiences she had. At times she would see the Christ Child in the halls of the monastery or have visions of angels. She also had a curiosity about ongoing private revelations, some of which were not approved by the Church. Certainly, Mother Angelica accepted whatever verdict the Church would offer on supposed revelations. But the role of mystics was always prevalent in her life. As a young girl, she met Rhoda Wise, a woman who had spiritual visions of Jesus and the saints, and at times bore the wounds of Jesus on her body.

One mystic above all, however, had a tremendous impact on Mother Angelica's life.

Mother was a sickly woman, often experiencing pain and numbness in her legs, which would affect her mobility. One day an alleged visionary who claimed to have been sent there by the Mother of God herself arrived at EWTN. The woman was named Paola Albertini, and she asked Mother Angelica to join her in praying the Rosary. Albertini most often communicated with Mary during the fourth decade of a mystery. As the two prayed together, Mother Angelica sensed God's desire to heal her. The visionary asked Mother Angelica if she could pray over her, and afterward she told Mother Angelica to remove her braces and walk. Mother Angelica felt a warmth in her legs as she began to walk. Gaining strength with every step, she progressed forward without braces or crutches. The healing did indeed take place and was confirmed by medical professionals.

Mother Angelica was in need of healing at a later time in her life. She suffered a stroke on Christmas Eve in 2001 that severely debilitated her. What were her options? She already had experienced an inexplicable healing while praying to an alleged mystic from Italy. This time, she put her hope in an approved apparition site of Our Lady, one known for miraculous healings: she was going to be a pilgrim to Lourdes, France. During one of her shows, Mother Angelica encouraged viewers to go to Lourdes, and even if the desired miracle did not result, she promised something spiritual would take place for that individual. As Mother Angelica processed around the sanctuary in Lourdes during one of the nightly processions, she held a candle high, and looking around, saw all the sick and knew it was for them she was to pray. She entered in their suffering and would offer her own suffering for them and witness to the world. The grace of the miracle she wanted did not come her way, but most certainly God rewarded His faithful servant with some spiritual gift.

At the age of eighty-one, Mother Angelica made a decision to travel to Japan to visit a monastery of religious sisters and meet with Church hierarchy about establishing an order of cloistered religious sisters there. During their sojourn, Mother Angelica and the accompanying sisters made the most of their trip by visiting the site of an apparition of Mary in Akita. The apparitions were received by Sr. Agnes Sasagawa, who would later bear the stigmata. A statue of Our Lady in the monastery spoke messages to Sr. Agnes beginning in 1973, and afterward the statue began to bleed, a phenomenon known to happen in rare circumstances. In recent years, the apparitions of Akita have gained popularity because one of the messages stated that bishops would oppose bishops, which arguably we are seeing in the Church today. The messages spoke of forthcoming chastisement and encouraged the visionary to offer her suffering in reparation for sin and to stay the anger of God. This message spoke to Mother Angelica because she knew suffering. In Akita, Mother Angelica offered her suffering to Jesus through the hands of Mary, and her suffering would only intensify as the years went by and death drew nearer.

Mother Angelica died on Easter Sunday, March 27, 2016, at the age of ninety-two. In her life, she did the will of God and listened for God's will in her prayer. This led her to the convent and eventually to founding her own monastery and a global Catholic television network. Through her own programs and writings, she shared her love for Mary and helped viewers to love Mary too. All she wanted was to help people know their faith and love their God. Mission accomplished.

How to Love Mary Like Mother Angelica

- Reflect on Mary's sorrow and suffering as she stood by the Cross of Jesus.
- Pray the Rosary using some of Mother Angelica's tips.
- Offer a prayer to the Blessed Mother, asking her to pray for someone you know who is sick and in need of healing.
- Learn more about Our Lady of Akita by reading a book or watching a documentary. Consider starting with the writings of Bob and Penny Lord.

Lesson 5

Relying on Mary's Prayers

Adele Brise

Adele Brise was born in Belgium on January 30, 1831. As a child, she was known for her religious fervor and piety. Her family's immigration to the United States in 1855 caused Adele consternation in the months prior to their departure. She recalled her childhood promise to the Virgin Mary at the time of her First Communion, a promise that entailed joining a religious community and working in the foreign missions. She sought the advice of her confessor in Belgium, who advised her to go to the United States; she could fulfill her promise there. Little did Adele know that the Virgin Mary would soon visit her and invite her to renew that promise, working in a new country and spreading the gospel.

After arriving in the United States in 1855, her parents, Lambert and Marie, acquired property in northeastern Wisconsin, where many Belgian immigrants had settled. The area quickly gained the name "Aux Premieres Belges," First Belgian Settlement. In her mid-twenties, with a meager education, Adele assisted her family in duties around the house and their farmland. Her work included carrying grain to the local grist mill. On a day like any other, Adele carried out her work. As she walked along the wooded trail to the grist mill with her sack of grain, a woman suddenly appeared between two trees, a maple and a hemlock. After a few moments, the mysterious woman vanished, without saying anything. Later that day, Adele shared what happened with her family, who did not discount the strange tale and instead suggested the visitor was a poor soul from Purgatory.

On the morning of Sunday, October 9, 1859, Adele, the pious and devout woman that she was, set out for Mass with her sister and a neighbor woman. The trek took them along the same wooded trail, and in the same place between the two trees, the woman appeared again. Only Adele saw her, though her friends knew something was happening. After Mass, Adele spoke to the priest about these events. He instructed her to ask the woman who she was and what she wanted. On her journey home, Adele did just that.

The woman appeared, for the third and final time. She was dressed all in white with a yellow sash around her waist and a crown of stars around her wavy golden hair. This time, she spoke, telling Adele, "I am the Queen of Heaven who prays for the conversion of sinners, and I wish you to do the same. You received Holy Communion this morning and that is well, but you must do more. Make a general confession and offer your Holy Communion for the conversion of sinners. If they do not convert and do penance, my Son will be obliged to punish them."

Mary, remembering Adele's promise made on the occasion of her First Communion, asked Adele, "What are you doing here in idleness while your companions are working in the vineyard of my Son?" Adele began to weep and responded, "What more can I do, dear Lady?" Her answer was: "Gather the children in this wild country and teach them what they should know for salvation."

"But how shall I teach them who know so little myself?" Adele asked. The Queen of Heaven responded, "Teach them their catechism, how to sign themselves with the sign of the Cross, and how to approach the sacraments; that is what I wish you to do. Go and fear nothing, I will help you."

It seems that the life of any soul who is graced with an apparition of Mary becomes defined by that miraculous event; it changes them in many ways. St. Juan Diego began to share the message of Our Lady of Guadalupe and gained converts by the millions. St. Bernadette withdrew from the world to pray for sinners. Sr. Lucia from Fatima reflected for years on her experiences, helping to promote devotion to the Immaculate Heart of Mary. For Adele Brise, Mary's three apparitions gave direction to her life. She received a mission and mandate from Heaven to pray and teach the children. And she spent the rest of her life fulfilling this request from Mary.

In the early years following the apparition, Adele would travel in a fifty-mile radius, knocking on the doors of strangers, doing household chores for them and in exchange teaching the children their catechism. Several years later she founded a lay tertiary (third order) group of women. They wore habits and called one another Sister. Eventually, a school was built, and the sisters taught the children on the very grounds where Mary gave the mandate to gather the children. Mary's apparitions to Adele changed her life, and by extension, they change us and call us to mission and action.

Mary's parting words to Adele were: "Go and fear nothing, I will help you." From the mouth of the Queen of Heaven, Adele received the pledge of heavenly assistance, which she relied upon throughout her life. Adele needed help as she fulfilled the mission of teaching the children, walking the peninsula, and entering the homes of families and instructing the children. She needed Mary's help when only a few cents remained in the money bag or when they were short on food. And most especially, the sisters, schoolchildren, and many in the immediate vicinity relied on Mary's help on the night of the Peshtigo Fire, historically the largest and most devastating fire in U.S. history. (The Peshtigo Fire has been forgotten because it occurred on October 8, 1871—the same night as the Great Chicago Fire.)

The fire that ravaged the area of Peshtigo, Wisconsin, began to burn across the body of water that separated the two points, in the Door Peninsula. Many people lost their lives. Near my parish in Brussels, Wisconsin, is a historical site called Tornado Park, where many sought refuge in the field. Tragically, all but a few perished. As the fire consumed everything in sight, the Chapel of Our Lady of Good Help stood in its way. Many people prayed there that night, carrying a statue of Mary around the property, changing directions whenever the smoke became too much for them. God heard their prayers, sparing Mary's sanctuary and many lives.

Over the years since Mary appeared, it hasn't been only Adele who relied on Mary's intercession but many others who make their pilgrimage and ask her to intercede for their special intention. Hundreds of candles stand aglow, testifying to the prayers of visitors in need of Mary's help.

During my seminary years, I spent an entire summer in Quetzeltenango, Guatemala, at a Benedictine monastery, with the intention of learning Spanish. From time to time, I would pray the Liturgy of the Hours with the monks, but I also joined their high school seminary students for their Marian devotion. They would pray the Rosary on three days of the school week, and on the other two they would simply gather in the chapel and sing songs honoring the Virgin Mary. This was really my first experience of, as I call it, serenading the Virgin. My experience with other Marian movements, like Schoenstatt, has been similar, with a dedicated time to sing Marian hymns.

While my time in Guatemala was my first real experience of it, I knew from reading about the life of Sr. Adele Brise that this was a form of devotion she employed, for herself, the sisters, and the schoolchildren. Sr. Marie du Sacre Coeur shared her memory of Adele: "I remember well, when I was about eight years old, we would pray and sing hymns around the trees where the Blessed Virgin had appeared to Sr. Adele." Another, Sr. Pauline, recounted: "I knelt in the dear little Chapel and sang with Adele her favorite hymn in French, *Chantons le nom admirable de la Reine des Cieux.*"

In the spiritual tradition, pilgrimage to holy sites reminds us that we are a pilgrim in the world, making our own pilgrimage from earth to Heaven. For centuries Catholics have made pilgrimages to holy sites, whether to tombs of saints to venerate their relics or to honor the Mother of God at one of her many sanctuaries. Some of the most popular places of Marian pilgrimage are related to Marian apparitions. For years Americans have traveled to Lourdes or Fatima to visit such a place. While the National Shrine of Our Lady of Good Help has existed since 1859, it was not well known. With the 2010 approval of the apparition, the shrine has seen a surge in pilgrims. For those Americans who cannot afford a transatlantic pilgrimage, it is possible to visit a place of the same stature, where pilgrims have experienced graces through Mary's intercession.

When a person makes a pilgrimage to Champion, Wisconsin, they will sit in the school of Our Lady, and not only will Mary teach them, but Sr. Adele will be their teacher too. She will teach them by the testimony of her life and through the story of her apparition. She will teach them how to love Mary through song and reliance on her intercession and will introduce us to a title of Mary that has its own history, aside from the apparition—Our Lady of Good Help. Mary's apparition to Adele changed her life and helped her fall in love with the Lord and our Blessed Lady. Be a pilgrim and become a student in Our Lady's school with Adele as your teacher.

***

How to Love Mary Like Sr. Adele

- The next time you are in need of heavenly assistance, ask Our Lady to intercede for you. Rely on her prayers, just as Adele did throughout her life.
- Do you have a statue of Mary in your home? Gather the family sometime soon and pray the Rosary (like so many did on the night of the Peshtigo Fire), then afterward sing a Marian hymn, in imitation of Sr. Adele, who would sing songs to the Madonna. Serenade the Madonna with hymns like "Immaculate Mary," "Hail, Holy Queen," "Sing of Mary," "Hail Mary, Gentle Woman," or any other Marian song you might know.
- Pilgrims flock to the National Shrine of Our Lady of Good Help. They go to Confession, attend Mass, pray the Rosary, and seek Mary's intercession. Be one of those pilgrims. Make a road trip sometime in the next year and visit the place where Adele received a visit from the Queen of Heaven.
- Pray the Litany to Our Lady of Good Help (found in appendix 4).
- Do you have a favorite Marian hymn like Adele? If so, resolve to sing it every night. If not, find one!

Lesson 6

A Childlike Love for Mary

St. Thérèse of Lisieux

"St. Thérèse, please pick me a rose from the heavenly garden and send it to me as a message of your love."

These words have been prayed by Catholics for more than a century since St. Thérèse's death. Believers have asked St. Thérèse for a specific color of rose during a time of discernment and decision making. Statues of St. Thérèse adorn many churches throughout the world because of popular devotion. And many have read her spiritual classic and autobiography, *Story of a Soul.*

I'll be honest — it took me a long time to warm up to and appreciate St. Thérèse of Lisieux. Like many Catholics, I found her too saccharine for my tastes. She was a young teenager who seemed a bit whiny at times. I didn't understand her teaching about spiritual childhood and the "Little Way." And I wondered why she was a Doctor of the Church. I set her autobiography down for a few years and one day picked it up again while on a religious pilgrimage. I read the book with new eyes, and her religious experience began to touch my soul. Before I knew it, I had statues and images of St. Thérèse, and I was devouring other books about her life, including her exchanges with a seminarian, captured in the book *Maurice and Thérèse*. She quickly became a spiritual friend of mine, and her love for the priesthood made her a good intercessor for me as I pursued the priesthood—and now during my priesthood too.

St. Thérèse was born to Louis and Zélie Martin in 1873. The Martins raised a pious household, instilling a love for God, Mary, and the saints in the hearts of their daughters, all of whom would enter religious life. Thérèse knew from her early years that she wanted to be a nun, yet this desire was not realized as quickly as she had hoped. At one point in her childhood, Thérèse laid ill in bed for a long time, weak and with death looming. She turned to the intercession of Mary, and looking at the statue of Our Lady in her room, asked Mary to hear her pleas. At that very moment, she said:

> The Blessed Virgin appeared *beautiful* to me, so *beautiful* that never had I seen anything so attractive; her face was suffused with an ineffable benevolence and tenderness, but what penetrated to the very depths of my soul was the *"ravishing smile of the Blessed Virgin."* At that instant, all my pain disappeared, and two large tears glistened on my eyelashes, and flowed down my cheeks silently, but they were tears of unmixed joy.[11]

The statue at which Thérèse was gazing came to life and Mary smiled at her. It was the smile of a mother delighting in a devoted daughter. It was a smile that brought comfort and healing to Thérèse so that she could persevere in life and follow the vocation of love to which God was calling her as a Carmelite sister.

[11] St. Thérèse of Lisieux, *Story of a Soul: A Study Edition* (Washington, DC: ICS Publications, 2005), 96.

Thérèse's desire to be a religious deepened as she grew in age. Her father planned to make a pilgrimage with the local diocese to Rome. It was Thérèse's wish to accompany her papa and to ask the Holy Father for permission to enter Carmel at such a young age, because she had not yet reached the minimum age for entry. During this pilgrimage, Thérèse had another Marian moment at a church in Paris. In her autobiography, she remarked after the Our Lady of the Smile healing: "I was not finding happiness again until I was kneeling at the feet of Our Lady of Victories."[12] Kneeling at the feet of Our Lady of Victories confirmed within the heart of Thérèse her belief that it was Our Lady who obtained the grace of her cure only a few years earlier. Thérèse recounts:

> I understood she was watching over me, that I was her child. I could no longer give her any other name but 'Mama' as this appeared ever so much more tender than mother. How fervently I begged her to protect me always, to bring to fruition as quickly as possible my dream of *hiding beneath the shadow of her virginal mantle!* This was one of my first desires as a child. When growing up, I understood it was at Carmel I would truly find the Blessed Virgin Mary's mantle, and toward this fertile Mount I directed all my desires. I prayed Our Lady of Victories to keep far from me everything that could tarnish my purity.[13]

This pilgrimage was a time of intense prayer for Thérèse. She continued to prepare her heart to receive all the graces God would give to her. She surrendered all her desires to Jesus through Mary at this altar of Our Lady of Victories. She requested of Mary

---

[12] St. Thérèse, *Story of a Soul*, 97.
[13] St. Thérèse, *Story of a Soul*, 192.

simple petitions of protection. As a little child, she stood before her mother, asking for all she could with the confidence that her heavenly mama would help her.

The pilgrimage group that Thérèse and her father were a part of were privileged to have an audience with the Holy Father. This was Thérèse's moment to ask for permission to enter Carmel. While instructed not to speak to the Holy Father, Thérèse did indeed make her request, and the Holy Father advised her to honor whatever the local bishop and Mother Superior instructed. Thérèse never relented in her desire for religious life, and she was granted permission to enter the Carmel of Lisieux. When the time came for her to profess her religious vows, her invitation began in this way: "God Almighty, Creator of Heaven and Earth, Sovereign Ruler of the Universe, and the Most Glorious Virgin Mary, Queen of the Heavenly Court, announce to you the Spiritual Espousals of Their August Son, Jesus, King of kings, and Lord of lords, with little Thérèse Martin."[14] In her vows, Thérèse became spiritually espoused to Jesus, the son of Mary, adding a new dimension to her relationship to Mary. She already knew Our Lady's role in Carmel, and as a consecrated cloistered religious she would continue to understand Mary's role in her vocation. She realized, "The Blessed Virgin shows me she is not displeased with me, for she never fails to protect me as soon as I invoke her. If some disturbance overtakes me, some embarrassment, I turn very quickly to her and as the most tender of Mothers she always takes care of my interests. How many times, when speaking to the novices, has it happened that I invoked her and felt the benefits of her motherly protection."[15] Mary comes to the aid of her daughter whenever she calls upon her.

[14] St. Thérèse, *Story of a Soul*, 263.
[15] St. Thérèse, *Story of a Soul*, 385.

When St. Thérèse made her First Confession, the priest told her to love Mary and strive to double her affection for her. Thérèse did just that, and she saw how Mary loved her as a child. She made an act of consecration to Mary, asking her to watch over her, a petition she would repeat throughout her life. She is often referred to as the Little Flower. As a child, she fashioned crowns for Mary, and later in life all she desired was to be a flower in Mary's crown. After a short life, lived as a cloistered Carmelite nun in Lisieux, France, having earned her crown of eternal life, she was able to see her heavenly Mother again, and enjoy the smile of Our Lady in the presence of our God forever.

How to Love Mary Like St. Thérèse

• The statue of Our Lady of the Smile, before which Thérèse prayed often, played a significant role in her life. Close your eyes and meditate on Our Lady's smile. What brought a smile to her as she spent her life with Jesus? Imagine Mary smiling at you right now. Why is she smiling at you?

• What names do you use to call upon Mary? Thérèse used quite a familiar way, calling her Mama. Try addressing Mary in less formal ways just as you are bringing to her petitions like St. Thérèse.

• How does Mary inspire you in your vocation?

Lesson 7

Catechesis about Mary Impacted Her Life

St. Kateri Tekakwitha

I needed a job back in the summer of 2008, and the opportunity opened up for me to work as a camp counselor at a summer camp named Camp Tekakwitha, in the Diocese of Green Bay. I didn't know much about this young saint and I don't think I learned much about her that summer. Her image did adorn the walls of the chapel and the dining room. Maybe we added the words "pray for us" after the mention of her name. When I worked at the camp, she was only a blessed, and not yet a saint. She was canonized in 2012. In time, St. Kateri would become one of my most powerful allies in the spiritual life.

Kateri Tekakwitha is sometimes called the Lily of the Mohawks. She was a Native American, born to a Christian Algonquin mother and a Mohawk chief in 1656. When she was only four years old, her parents and a brother died from smallpox, and Kateri survived with some scarring and partial blindness. The Jesuit missionaries arrived and began to teach the Natives about God, the Gospels, and their prayers. Kateri received the gospel with much joy and enthusiasm because she had known a little from her Christian mother. She requested Baptism and was initiated into the Catholic Faith in

1676. Kateri was not shy about her faith with her fellow people, and contrary to the wishes of her relatives, she did not want to marry. Continued persecution forced Kateri to flee that village and take up refuge near Montreal, where she could freely practice her faith.

Kateri felt called to the virginal life and today is recognized by the Church as a patroness of consecrated virgins. This love and desire for virginity was, in part, inspired by the Blessed Virgin Mary. According to one of Kateri's biographers, Fr. Claude Chauchetière, "The virginity that Katharine [Kateri] always loved, that she preserved at the cost of her bodily life, was the reason of her frequent recourse to the Blessed Virgin; for she regarded her life as a model to be imitated as much as possible."[16] She was so much in love with God that she wanted to dedicate her entire life to single-hearted devotion to our Savior.

One way in which Kateri became familiar with the virginity of Mary was through the Litany of the Blessed Mother, or the Litany of Loreto, in which Mary is saluted as Queen of Virgins. This Marian prayer became for Kateri a little catechism about the Blessed Mother as it related her motherly and regal titles along with others. Kateri memorized many prayers, and the Litany of the Blessed Mother was one of them that she recited each evening after the common prayers in her cabin.

Kateri learned other Marian prayers. She was dedicated to the Angelus prayer, which is recited three times a day, at six in the morning, noon, and six in the evening. The praying of the Angelus is a recalling of the angel's announcement to Mary and the Incarnation of Christ as the Word became flesh. Part of the Angelus also includes the repeating of Mary's fiat: "Let it be done to me according to your

---

[16] Lynn Marie Busch, "The Marian Spirituality of Saint Kateri Tekakwitha (1656–1680)," *Marian Studies* 62 (2011): 18.

word." As Kateri strived to live her life in imitation of the Blessed Mother, the Angelus was a reminder to her of doing God's will.

Kateri also prayed the Rosary fervently. Like St. Padre Pio, she was never seen without a rosary, and it's said that, often when praying it, she would add a simultaneous penitential practice. Kateri also held in high regard Saturdays, a day traditionally associated with the Blessed Mother and her closeness to Christ's tomb on Holy Saturday. On these days, Kateri would try to undertake a special act of mortification as a sign of her love, observe the day with Marian prayer, and imitate the virtues of Mary. Kateri also had a deep devotion to the Passion of Jesus. She carved a cross on a tree and would spend countless hours in prayer contemplating the love of Christ. No doubt the Sorrowful Mother who stood by the Cross also played a part in Kateri's reflection.

I think back to those days at Camp Tekakwitha, and I remember two siblings who were homesick during the week. Being the counselor who was religious and devotional, I was asked if I would pray the Rosary with the children each night. There we sat, in front of the statue of Mary, and reflected on the life of Jesus and Mary. It was a simple practice, but looking back now it was done in imitation of St. Kateri Tekakwitha. If you don't have Marian prayers memorized, learn them, commit them to memory and pray them often. Doing so led St. Kateri Tekakwitha, in her short life, to love Mary and to want to imitate her.

How to Love Mary Like St. Kateri Tekakwitha

• Kateri learned the Litany of Loreto and was inspired by the title Queen of Virgins. Is there a title that inspires you and can impact your life? If you are a mother, look

at the Mother titles and see if there is one that you can
imitate.

• Is there a certain Marian prayer or litany that you have a
special love for? If so, resolve to say it every week, or even
every day.

• Pray the Angelus each day. Try to do so three times a
day—in the morning, at noon, and in the evening.

• How can you keep Saturday in honor of Our Lady? Think
of a practical way to always be reminded of Mary's presence on her special day of the week.

Lesson 8

Streams of Grace

St. Faustina Kowalska

As I discerned my priestly vocation, there were a few options before me. The straightforward option was to become a diocesan
priest for the Diocese of Green Bay, meaning that I would serve
as a parish priest. In my late high school years and during college,
when I returned to the idea of a priestly vocation, I explored the
possibility of a religious community called the Marians of the Immaculate Conception.

Their vocation director was a vocal promoter of Marian devotion and had an incredible story of Marian conversion and vocation. I was attracted to the order's charism, which included
fostering Marian devotion, promotion of Divine Mercy, and praying
for the poor souls in Purgatory. The Marians of the Immaculate
Conception were closely linked with the Divine Mercy devotion
as they were given a copy of St. Faustina's diary and the directive
to spread the message and devotion. The Divine Mercy novena,
chaplet, and special Sunday each year holds a special place in the
devotional life of modern Catholics.

St. Faustina's diary, *Divine Mercy in My Soul*, might be a little
daunting for some people because of its length. Throughout the

diary, the presence of Mary in St. Faustina's revelations and her personal devotion are expressed. For those drawn to Divine Mercy, Mary is also worthy of our devotion, for she is the Mother of Mercy.

Born Helena Kowalska in 1905, Faustina became the secretary of Divine Mercy. She believed she had a religious vocation from a young age. She began having mystical experiences in her late teenage years. One experience was at a dance, when she heard Jesus speak to her. That experience compelled her to seriously discern her vocation and leave everything to follow Jesus. Because she was poor, several orders turned her down. The Congregation of the Sisters of Our Lady of Mercy accepted her and allowed her entrance. In 1931, she began to receive apparitions of Jesus, who would reveal the devotion to her and whose words she recorded in her diary. The message spread with the help of her spiritual director, Blessed Fr. Michael Sopocko. Faustina died of tuberculosis in 1938. The devotion gained much popularity under the papacy of Pope St. John Paul II, a Polish pope, who beatified and canonized this Polish nun.

In addition to the mystical experiences with Jesus that St. Faustina experienced, her diary recounts many experiences with the Blessed Virgin Mary. Often, she wrote that she saw or heard Our Lady and that she would talk to her. In moments of uncertainty, St. Faustina would simply pray, "Mary, lead me, guide me."[17] Mary would communicate with St. Faustina. For example, on one occasion, she says, "The Blessed Mother was telling me to accept all that God asked of me like a little child, without question; otherwise it would not be pleasing to God."[18] These little

[17] St. Faustina, *Divine Mercy in My Soul* (Stockbridge, MA: Marian Press, 2005), paragraph 11.
[18] St. Faustina, *Divine Mercy*, paragraph 526.

lessons from the Blessed Mother made her one of St. Faustina's many teachers.[19]

St. Faustina was also aware of Mary's role in mediating grace. She realized that it was through Our Lady that streams of grace flowed out for the world.[20] In 1929, when St. Faustina renewed her vows to the Lord, she saw Jesus, who placed a golden girdle around her waist. This grace of purity was something that St. Faustina realized was obtained for her by Our Lady.[21] In another teaching of Our Lady, St. Faustina learned that the virtues closest to the heart of Mary were humility, purity, and love of God.[22] Since these virtues were contained within Our Lady, St. Faustina desired to imitate them and deepen them in her own life. St. Faustina would also beg Our Lady for these graces and many others, including that of fidelity. She writes, "I earnestly begged the Mother of God to obtain for me the grace of fidelity to these inner inspirations of faithfully carrying out God's will."[23]

Feast days were very important in the spiritual life of St. Faustina. She would prepare for them by novenas and greater dedication to prayer. On one occasion, Jesus asked St. Faustina to pray a novena, uniting her heart with Mary for nine days.[24] One year, for the feast of the Immaculate Conception, she recounts, she "prepared not only by means of the novena said in common by the whole community, but I also made a personal effort to salute Her a thousand times each day, saying a thousand 'Hail Marys'

[19] St. Faustina refers to Mary as an Instructress in paragraph 620 and communicates another teaching from Mary in paragraph 1711.
[20] St. Faustina, *Divine Mercy*, paragraph 1746.
[21] St. Faustina, *Divine Mercy*, paragraph 40.
[22] St. Faustina, *Divine Mercy*, paragraph 1414.
[23] St. Faustina, *Divine Mercy*, paragraph 170.
[24] St. Faustina, *Divine Mercy*, paragraph 32.

for nine days in Her praise."²⁵ That is intense preparation. One
thousand Hail Marys! Sometimes we struggle to say only fifty-three
a day through the Rosary. This novena of a thousand Hail Marys
was repeated by her several times throughout her life, including one
time when she was ill. On other occasions, her Marian devotion
was as simple as saying one Hail Mary to obtain interior peace.

St. Faustina understood the richness of God's mercy because
Jesus revealed this message to her. But she also learned many lessons
in the spiritual life from the Blessed Virgin. She knew that Mary
could obtain many graces for her. She experienced this through
her simple conversations and, at other times, intense preparation.
Let us listen to how Mary speaks to us and let us be confident that
she will obtain many graces for us from her Son.

How to Love Mary Like St. Faustina

- If you saw Mary, what do you think she would say to you?
- Beg Mary for a specific grace, whether it is purity, fidelity,
  humility, or love of God.
- Figure out the next major feast of Our Lady and con-
  sciously prepare for it each day with a set prayer or no-
  vena. Some common feasts you can prepare for are the
  Immaculate Conception (December 8), Mary, Mother of
  God (January 1), and the Assumption (August 15).
- Pray one of these prayers from St. Faustina's diary:

  *Mary, my Mother and my Lady, I offer You my soul, my
  body, my life and my death, and all that will follow it. I*

²⁵ St. Faustina, *Divine Mercy*, paragraph 1412.

place everything in Your hands. O my Mother, cover my soul with Your virginal mantle and grant me the grace of purity of heart, soul, and body. Defend me with Your power against all enemies, and especially against those who hide their malice behind the mask of virtue. O lovely lily! You are for me a mirror, O my Mother![26]

Mary, Immaculate Virgin, take me under Your special protection and guard the purity of my soul, heart, and body. You are the model and star of my life.[27]

O pure Virgin, pour courage into my heart and guard it.[28]

---

[26] St. Faustina, *Divine Mercy*, paragraph 79.
[27] St. Faustina, *Divine Mercy*, paragraph 874.
[28] St. Faustina, *Divine Mercy*, paragraph 915.

Lesson 9

Dedicated to and Protected by Mary

Archbishop Fulton J. Sheen

Many American Catholics are familiar with Archbishop Fulton Sheen. He was a notable figure of American Catholicism for decades due to his zeal in proclaiming the gospel. His program, *Life Is Worth Living*, aired on prime-time television and earned him an Emmy nomination. It also appeared on EWTN, since I grew up in a home with my grandmother, you can imagine I heard my fair share of Archbishop Sheen. While I was in college seminary, I asked Fulton Sheen's intercession because he was a great philosopher and I was ... not.

One of his books, *The Priest Is Not His Own*, is highly recommended reading for a man in the seminary. In college seminary, I could never get into the writing of Sheen—not even his book entirely devoted to the Blessed Virgin Mary, *The World's First Love*. It wasn't until major seminary, when I decided to write a paper on the spirituality of Fulton Sheen, that I began to appreciate his wit and wisdom. What changed? I read his autobiography, which allowed me to get to know him. After knowing who he was as a person, I could hear his voice in his writing.

How They Love Mary

Families strongly devoted to the Blessed Virgin will ask her maternal care and protection for their child on the day he is baptized. The mother and father will present the child to Our Lady in front of a statue or by laying the child on the Mary altar. They might offer a prayer similar to this: "Mary, I offer you my child, I ask you to protect him. I consecrate this child to you and pray he might always do God's will." Afterward, some other Marian prayer might be prayed.

This is exactly what Newton and Delia Sheen did. They took baby Fulton to the altar and entrusted him to the prayers of Our Lady. All through his life, Fulton would know of the powerful prayers and protection of the Blessed Virgin Mary.

Ordained in 1919, he would fulfill this promise and go on to preach and share about the Virgin Mary throughout his ministry as a priest and bishop. Sheen believed that Our Lady was necessary for the priest because, though a celibate man, a priest could not live without love, so Mary fills up the need for feminine love. She brings fruitfulness in the midst of virginity. Mary intercedes for the priest in his weakness and his needs. Mary teaches the priest how to live, and her life of virtue becomes a model for him to follow.

Indeed, just as the beginning of his life started with an act of Marian consecration, so, too, did his priesthood. Fulton Sheen often remarked that two things made his priesthood successful: a daily holy hour spent in prayer before the Blessed Sacrament and, every Saturday, a Mass celebrated in honor of Our Lady to give thanks for his priesthood and to ask for her protection.

On the occasion of his fifth anniversary of priestly ordination, Fulton Sheen engaged in a form of Marian devotion that was a part of his priestly life: pilgrimage. He visited the apparition site of Lourdes, where, in 1858, the saintly Bernadette Soubirous saw the Blessed Mother and uncovered a spring of healing water. Sheen,

56

who at the time was a graduate student in Belgium, had limited funds available for the pilgrimage. He had enough to pay for the train ticket but not enough for a hotel room. He told Our Lady that she would have to pay the bill. Trusting in divine providence, he booked one of the more expensive hotels in Lourdes and planned to stay for nine days. As he was preparing to leave Lourdes, with no money yet to pay this bill, he visited the grotto to say goodbye to Our Lady. As he left the grotto and was walking back to the hotel, a gentleman asked him if he spoke French. Sheen did. The man asked him if he would be willing to accompany his group to Paris and act as a translator for them. Sheen agreed. Then the man asked him, "Have you paid your hotel bill yet?" Sheen quickly responded, indicating he had not. This man was going to take care of it. It took until the last hour before he left, but Our Lady came through in the end.

After telling this story in one of his talks, Sheen remarked that he returned to Belgium with much more than he started out with. The family probably paid him a stipend to travel to Paris, so literally he had more money than when he left for Lourdes. But he returned with much more spiritually as well. A greater trust in God and the intercession of Our Lady was his. During his lifetime, Sheen visited Lourdes over thirty times. And each time he continued to receive grace in abundance.

In his talks, Sheen offered a myriad of advice pertaining to the fostering of a Marian devotion. He encouraged keeping a statue or image of Our Lady in your bedroom and saying a prayer each day before it. For a devotee of Mary already, he encouraged the recitation of the Little Office of Our Lady. Sheen also promoted the daily recitation of the Rosary. Some folks complain that the Rosary is repetitive, but as Fulton Sheen reminds us, we tell some people we love them every day, over and over—and we mean it.

How They Love Mary

So, too, with the Rosary. He also pointed out that when you pray the Hail Mary during the Rosary, you don't think about the prayer being prayed, but you think about the mystery being meditated. The Hail Mary becomes the vehicle by which meditation occurs.

Sheen also recommended a book on the rosary by a Protestant believer; it is titled *Five for Sorrow, Ten for Joy: Meditations on the Rosary*, by J. Neville Ward.

Finally, we might seem accomplished when we pray five decades or one set of mysteries. In his talks, Sheen encouraged the recitation of fifteen mysteries a day. (This was before Pope St. John Paul II promulgated the Luminous Mysteries.) He told his listeners that they didn't need to say the Rosary on their knees, but that it could be an ambulatory prayer. Pray a decade or two while driving to work or waiting at the supermarket. Carry the rosary with you as you walk from place to place and pray a decade. He firmly believed we always had time for one or two decades, and by praying a few at a time, you would be able to pray all the mysteries in a day.

Another form of Marian devotion he promoted was entrusting to Our Lady the conversion of individuals for whom we are praying. He believed Our Lady always obtained the conversion of souls for whom he prayed. Sheen worked with several individuals, including celebrities, to bring them into full communion with the Catholic Church. On one of his trips to Lourdes, Sheen prayed that he might be inconvenienced to save a soul. When he was leaving the grotto one evening, he was followed back to his hotel by a young pilgrim. Sheen asked the pilgrim why she was following him. She told him that she believed maybe he could help her. She was an unbeliever, visiting the Pyrenees (where Lourdes is located) with a group of atheists. All her companions were on a bus trip, but she chose to stay behind and visit Lourdes. Sheen spent a few days with the young girl, teaching her the Faith, and eventually she requested to be reconciled with the Church. Later, Sheen learned that all the girl's friends died when their bus crashed. She was the only survivor—and now, a believer. Our Lady obtains the grace of conversion for people. Sheen captured this best with his wit when telling this joke: Jesus was talking with St. Peter and mentioned to him that it seemed a lot of people were being admitted to Heaven. He asked St. Peter why he wasn't vetting the new arrivals. Peter said that every time he closed the door, Mary would open a window. Indeed, Mary opens the window so that unbelievers and sinners can become believers and repent of their sins.

Fulton Sheen loved the Blessed Mother. She is "the world's first love"—the dream of God from the beginning of creation. Sheen also believed that Mary would keep people faithful to the Church. If there was an absence of love for the Church, there was an absence of loving Mary. With Mary, he said that one would never lose their soul. Like Archbishop Fulton Sheen, let us love the Blessed Virgin Mary because if we are dedicated to her, we will definitely know of her protection.

How to Love Mary Like Archbishop Fulton Sheen

- Find a Saturday Mass and attend it, knowing that you are doing so to honor Our Lady.
- You, too, can visit Lourdes. They have a webcam that allows you to see the Grotto. Visit their website and make a virtual visit.
- Use a Rosary meditation book to enhance your prayer and deepen your meditation. You may also wish to read Sheen's *Life of Christ*, allowing his reflections pertinent to the Rosary mysteries to inform your prayer.

- If you have never prayed a complete (all the mysteries) Rosary in one day, try the methods recommended by Archbishop Sheen and see if you are able to do it.
- If you are praying for the conversion of someone you love, ask Our Lady to obtain the grace of conversion for them. Pray the Rosary for that intention. Offer your Holy Communion for the grace of their conversion.

A Love for Mary's Many Names

Mother Mary Francis, PCC

During my four years at Mundelein Seminary, I became familiar with the Institute on Religious Life (IRL) and attended their annual events. I was no stranger to the IRL; with my own discernment in high school, I became familiar with their work and annual confer-ence and longed to be a part of it. It wasn't until seminary that I would fulfill that desire, and now as a priest I have been a speaker there. The presence of the consecrated religious on campus always lifted my spirits. If I was in a spiritual funk, their joyful witness would lift me out of it. Similar to my experience in Canada, the IRL would sponsor an all-night prayer vigil after their Saturday evening program. I always attended and was moved by the expression of their love for God. What I saw encouraged me to love Jesus more.

In college seminary, I encountered a spiritual writer, a cloistered religious who would have a significant impact on me. I spent a lot of time in the library when I was in college seminary. I could often be found camped out at a table working on a research paper. The library at Conception Seminary College had a table where they would put out new books and seasonal books that they pulled from the shelves. As I passed by the table one day as Advent approached,

How They Love Mary

I encountered an author who would become significant in my spiritual life. Her name was Mother Mary Francis, a Poor Clare Colettine abbess from Roswell, New Mexico.

I had an affinity for the Poor Clares because I knew someone who entered the Poor Clare Colettines in Rockford, Illinois. I had visited the monastery a few times. Once when I was in Rockford, I rang the bell and asked the cloistered nun on the other end if I could pray in the chapel. She told me, "Jesus would like that very much." After I was ordained a priest, in the few weeks between ordination and starting at my first assignment, I was able to celebrate Mass for the nuns in Rockford. St. Francis of Assisi had a close associate, St. Clare, who founded the women's branch of the Franciscans. In the 1400s—about two hundred years after their founding—St. Colette of Corbie felt called to reform the order to a life more focused on poverty and austerity.

My love for consecrated religious and connection to the Poor Clares was a match for me as I selected Mother Francis's *Come Lord Jesus* as my Advent reading. I would later read her Lenten reflections, after priestly ordination. Often, I would use her wisdom as the foundation for my homily at daily Mass, and sometimes even on the weekend. The words of Mother Mary Francis were meant for cloistered, consecrated religious, but as a man pursuing God in seminary and later in my priestly spirituality, her musings found a home in my heart, leading me to deeper meditation and love of God. And what I found in her writings also told me she was a woman who loved Mary.

Mother Mary Francis, born on Valentine's Day in 1921, with the name Alberta, lived her early life in St. Louis. She set off to join the Poor Clares in the Chicagoland area, where she wrote poetry with the permission of Mother Abbess. Her writing quickly attracted the admiration of (among many others) Hilaire Belloc, who sent his daughter to America expressly to meet the young nun. Devotion to Our Lady was instilled in her religious name, as she would be called Mother Mary Francis of Our Lady throughout her consecrated life. Upon her final profession of vows, she was sent as one of the founding sisters of the Roswell, New Mexico, monastery and would be elected Mother Abbess in 1964. She would serve in this capacity until 2005. During her time as Mother Abbess, she was responsible for the spiritual formation and care of the religious community. One such responsibility included giving spiritual reflections for the edification of the nuns. These reflections would be published in several books by Ignatius Press. Her Marian reflections were published as *Cause of Our Joy: Walking Day by Day with Our Lady*. This book, along with additional resources provided to me by the nuns in Roswell, informed my knowledge of Mother Mary Francis's Marian devotion.

After reading her writings, I realized that her devotion to Mary centered on one specific prayer. Like St. Kateri, Mary Francis had a deep love for the Litany of Loreto. The foreword to *Cause of Our Joy*, authored by the Roswell nuns who knew her, said that she would offer the Litany of Our Lady daily especially for a particular sister who might have been undergoing a trial or difficulty. With the Litany of Our Lady, Mother Mary Francis entrusted the nuns to Our Lady, asking her under her many titles to pray for them.

Cause of Our Joy also begins with a series of reflections on various titles of Our Lady that come from the Litany. Mother Mary Francis reflected on these titles and shared the treasure of meditation with the sisters. Finally, even when Mother Francis delivered a meditation on a specific feast day, she often would focus her meditation on a title of Our Lady. On the feast of Mary, Mother of God, she offered her thoughts on Mary as the Refuge of Sinners, Queen of the World, and Help of Christians. On the feast of Mary's Queenship, she turned to the Litany of Loreto again, examining Mary's queenly title. Given her life as a consecrated religious, she chose to offer her meditation on Mary as Queen of Virgins. Throughout her life, Mother Mary Francis meditated and invoked the many titles of Our Lady.

Mother Mary Francis spoke and wrote about Mary in the context of cloistered religious life to sisters who lived with her in the cloister. Her meditations are now read by people outside of the cloister, who can gain tremendous benefit from her thought. She had the ability to relate Mary on a personal level, communicating what the example of Mary's life means for our experience of Christianity today. She knew that Mary sought to do the will of God daily in her life, leading her to remind us that "Our Lady never deviated from God's will but continued straight forward."[29]

In our life, then, we too should seek to do God's will, never straying from it, persevering on the path God has set us. When we are perplexed by what God's will might be or by what we should do next, Mother Mary Francis offers the following spiritual counsel: "Think of Our Lady, what she would have done. Ask Our Lady to help you."[30]

The Blessed Virgin has preceded us on our earthly journey. She lived a life of virtue and models that for us. Mary also lived her life in close relationship with God. Looking to Mary as a model and teacher, Mother Mary Francis encourages us to "look to Our Lady to teach [you] this relationship with God."[31]

[29] Mother Mary Francis, PCC, *Cause of Our Joy* (San Francisco: Ignatius, 2018), 77–78.
[30] Mother Mary Francis, *Cause of Our Joy*, 15.
[31] Mother Mary Francis, *Cause of Our Joy*, 136.

Another dimension of Mother Mary Francis's devotion to Mary was enriched by her prayerful meditation. In her prayer she would engage her meditation, and as she offers her own meditations it gives us subjects for our own prayerful consideration. She imagines, for example, at the birth of our Lord—that as Mary looked at the face of the child, surely the first word she said was Jesus.[32] She also considered Mary rocking the baby Jesus.[33] In her prayer, not only did she engage her imagination, but she also had a very personal way to approach Mary. Mother Mary Francis knew of the powerful intercession of Our Lady and encouraged her sisters not to be afraid to ask Mary's specific prayers.

"Let us pray to Our Lady for one another, that she who never violated her maternity by any unwillingness to suffer will help each of us to be a *mater inviolata*,"[34] she writes. "Let us ask Our Lady to be the gate of our hearts; let us allow her to be the gate, because if she is the gate, when her Son stands there knocking, that gate will swing wide open."[35]

We need not be afraid to approach Our Lady. Jesus gave her to us as a mother and she wants to pray for us, our needs, our families, friends, and whatever other petitions we bring to her attention. For this is what she did at Cana. Mary prayed with confidence,[36] and we should have that same confidence when invoking her intercession.

Mother Mary Francis lived out the majority of her cloistered religious life in a monastery dedicated to Our Lady of Guadalupe. Our Lady entrusted St. Juan Diego with the task of asking the

[32] Mother Mary Francis, *Cause of Our Joy*, 131.
[33] Mother Mary Francis, *Cause of Our Joy*, 151.
[34] Mother Mary Francis, *Cause of Our Joy*, 109.
[35] Mother Mary Francis, *Cause of Our Joy*, 198.
[36] "Our Lady's Prayer," a meditation received from the Poor Clares at Roswell.

bishop for a church to be built. That church would house the beautiful and miraculous image of Our Lady impressed upon Juan Diego's tilma. In her religious life, Mother Mary Francis built a shrine to Our Lady in her heart and soul, visiting, reflecting, and pondering over Our Lady's life and titles. The devotion of Mother Mary Francis to Mother Mary inspires us to love Mary through meditation and by calling upon her many names in the Litany of Loreto.

How to Love Mary Like Mother Mary Francis

• Pray the Litany of Loreto. As you pray it, what title of Mary do you relate to the most? Daily invoke that title of Mary. If it's Queen of Peace, after you pray in the morning or at the end of your Rosary, add "Queen of Peace, pray for us." Begin reflecting on the title, asking yourself, "What does this mean for my life?"

• Whenever you are making a decision, ask the question, "What would Jesus or Mary do? What would they think of this choice?"

• Whatever request or petition you have, don't be afraid simply to say, "Mary, please pray for this need of mine."

Lesson 11

Sincerity in Devotion

Fr. Lukas Etlin, OSB

I returned to the seminary in the fall of 2009 and began studies at a Benedictine Abbey in rural northwest Missouri. I had visited Conception Abbey and Seminary College the previous spring for an Encounter with God's Call event. Believing I was called to the priesthood, I felt that Conception Abbey was the right place to resume my studies. I enjoyed the rhythm of life, daily prayer, classes, and my peers. I settled in as a transfer junior with the idea of attending Conception Seminary for two years. I was able to get to know many of the monks. Some were my professors; others were fellow students. One day, a brother named Maximilian shared with me a story about a saintly monk from the abbey, Fr. Lukas Etlin.

The aura of sanctity surrounding this monk was so well known that at one point there was consideration of his cause for sainthood, and there was a prayer card asking his intercession. The front of the card included a picture of Fr. Lukas writing at his desk. Below were his dates, 1864–1927, and the words "Apostle of the Most Holy Eucharist." TAN Books republished, in 1999, a small tract by Fr. Lukas capturing his Eucharistic devotion, *The Holy Eucharist: Our All.* He wrote often about the Eucharist and spent long hours before the tabernacle in prayer. He would rise in the middle of the night to spend time before the Blessed Sacrament and would encourage his fellow religious in performing adoration and hourly spiritual communions.

Another love of Fr. Lukas was the Blessed Mother. So said the tract I read. So, too, did the prayer card Br. Maximilian gave me: "O God, you favored your servant, Father Lukas Etlin, with a deep love for your Son in the Mystery of the Holy Eucharist, for the Virgin Mother of Jesus, for the angels and the saints, and with apostolic charity for all." I've kept this prayer card in my breviary. During my time at Conception Abbey, I would pray it almost daily. This reminder in my breviary that I happen upon every now and again was enough for me to want to know more about Fr. Etlin's Marian devotion as a Benedictine monk.

Fr. Lukas was born to Aloysius and Barbara Etlin on February 28, 1864, in the village of Sarnen in Switzerland. He was baptized Augustine Alfred, but commonly went by Alfred before his entrance into religion. His hometown was known for the saintly Blessed Nicholas de Flue, a hermit who was considered a distant relative of the Etlins. He received his First Holy Communion in 1874 and was confirmed a year later. He was educated at the Benedictine College of Engelberg, and there he became a member of the Sodality of Our Lady, the beginning of his tender love for the Blessed Virgin Mary. In his spiritual life, he fostered a devotion to St. Gertrude and St. Mechtilde, both Benedictine nuns. He also frequently meditated on Christ's Passion, finding spiritual nourishment in the reading of Bl. Anne Catherine Emmerich's *The Dolorous Passion of Our Lord Jesus Christ*. In school at Engelberg, Alfred became familiar with the monastic way of life and the stirring of a vocation was surfacing in his soul. He had a great passion and skill as an artist, which could have been his career. Not knowing what to do, he turned to Our

Lady, kneeling at her altar, and entrusted his vocation to Mary; he believed he should sacrifice fame and fortune and become a Benedictine monk. It would have been easy for Alfred to enter the Engelberg Abbey, but instead he chose to go to America and join the newly formed monastery—a "daughter" of Engelberg—in the rolling hills of Missouri. That, of course, was Conception Abbey. After entering the monastery, Alfred was given a new name and was forever called Lukas, after the artist St. Luke, who allegedly painted a holy image of the Blessed Virgin Mary.

This son of Our Lady was ordained a priest on August 15, 1891, the solemnity of Our Lady's Assumption. His devotion to the Holy Eucharist was very evident. After he celebrated his first Mass, he remained in prayer for several hours at the foot of the altar. On March 17, 1892, Fr. Lukas was appointed the chaplain of the neighboring Benedictine nuns, down the road from Conception in Clyde, Missouri. For the remainder of his life and priesthood, except when he returned to Switzerland to recuperate after an episode of bad health, he would celebrate Mass daily for the nuns and offer benediction.

On the walls of Fr. Lukas's room was a large crucifix and a beautiful image of Our Lady of the Sacred Heart. Those who knew Fr. Lukas commented on how he gazed at the image with a childlike love and confidence. He would often kiss the image of Mary in his coming and going. Sometimes when he would be in conversation with someone, he would direct them to the image and say how lovely Mary looked.[37] In his priestly ministry, he would begin a periodical called *Tabernacle and Purgatory*. He would present each issue to Our Lady and offer three Hail Marys for all who would

---

[37] Rt. Rev. Dr. Norbert Weber, OSB, *Father Lukas Etlin, OSB: A Short Biography* (Clyde, MO: Benedictine Convent of Perpetual Adoration, 1931), 54.

read it. Through the periodical, he would also fundraise to help European seminaries and religious orders pay for the formation of their students. When he would send out letters asking for money or dispensing funds, he would entrust the envelope to the image of Mary and say his three Hail Marys. Sometimes he would also offer the plea, "O sweetest Mother, help them."[38]

By reciting the Rosary, Fr. Lukas experienced Mary's protection in dangerous situations while he was traveling. He knew the grace of Mary's prayers and was moved to thanksgiving. He often commented, "The Blessed Virgin Mary is so good to me! I almost have to ask her to withhold the vehemence of the love that floods my soul."[39] While never investigated, Fr. Lukas admitted that the Blessed Mother visited him a few times and conversed with him. Given his deep love and devotion, this should not surprise us. The Church acknowledges that there could be many souls who have had heavenly visitations about which we will never know.

In his spiritual life, after his devotion to the Eucharist, Mary was his second love. He did see connections between Mary and the Eucharist because we adore God in her. He once taught that, during the celebration of the Mass, the three swings of the thurible (when incense is used) should be a moment of personal prayer glorifying "the Sacred Heart of Jesus in the Holy Eucharist with the purity, the humility, and the love of the Blessed Virgin Mary."[40]

One of the principal points Fr. Lukas brought out in his Marian preaching was to have sincerity and authenticity in one's devotion to Mary. It was evident from his own expressed devotion that he was sincere in his love for Mary. On the feast of the Holy Rosary,

---

[38] Weber, *Short Biography*, 53.
[39] Weber, *Short Biography*, 50.
[40] Weber, *Short Biography*, 30.

October 7, 1923, he preached on the difference between exterior and interior devotion. He said, "Let us not be satisfied with our exterior practice of devotion to the Blessed Virgin Mary. Let us not even be satisfied with our Rosary we pray daily to the Mother of God, because this is an exterior practice." The exterior for him was not enough. It must touch the interior life. In a question posed for reflection, he asks, "Am I still a stranger to the Blessed Virgin Mary? ... Is Mary the sweetness, the life, the joy of my life, or am I still a stranger? Do I forget her? Must I confess that I do not experience special joy on her feast days?" Earlier in 1923, on the feast of the Annunciation, he brought this theme to the attention of the nuns of Clyde as well. He began the homily: "Frequently we should ask and examine ourselves regarding our devotion, our sentiments, our love toward the Blessed Virgin Mary." In that same homily, he drew upon his beloved St. Mechtilde and a mystical vision she had of the angels and the power of the angelic salutation. This led Fr. Lukas to encourage reciting the Hail Mary throughout the day, not just during the Rosary but before and after Holy Communion, before the tabernacle, and at other times throughout the day.

Fr. Lukas believed and preached that we should love Mary. Loving Mary has tremendous benefits for the devotee because Mary leads us to holiness. It is also a means by which we obtain grace from God. Fr. Lukas said, "There is no easier way to attain the Kingdom of Heaven and obtain graces from God in abundance than a tender love for the Blessed Virgin Mary."[41] In another homily, he says, "We know that by loving the Blessed Virgin Mary tenderly we will obtain the love of Jesus Christ."[42] Those who love Mary also strive to imitate her virtues.

[41] Homily, Feast of the Holy Rosary, 1923.
[42] Homily, Feast of the Annunciation, 1923.

In his 1924 Annunciation homily, he outlines imitation of Mary's virginal glory (which for married couples we could translate to purity and chastity), humility, and ardent love of God and union with His will. Fr. Lukas Etlin shows us not only how to love Mary but *why* we should love Mary.

Fr. Lukas Etlin died in a car accident on December 16, 1927. He was on his way to St. Joseph, Missouri, to pick up some items for the liturgical celebration of Christmas. Before departing with his driver, he kissed his picture of the Blessed Virgin, not knowing that the prayer he prayed so often would reach fulfillment that day: "Pray for us sinners now and at the hour of our death." He repeated the Hail Mary so often and taught others to do so with great devotion. In death, he now was able to see the Blessed Virgin, show her his love and affection, and join her and the angels and saints in the worship of our Triune God in the Kingdom of Heaven.

How to Love Mary Like Fr. Lukas Etlin, OSB

- Visit a Mary altar at a local church and kneel in prayer.
- Have you ever kissed your favorite picture or statue of Mary? If you haven't, give it a try!
- Entrust your correspondences in writing to the Blessed Mother's intercession. Pray a Hail Mary for whomever you are sending a text, e-mail, or letter to.
- Examine your exterior and interior devotion to Mary. How can you love her more sincerely and authentically?
- Say the Hail Mary intentionally with a deep amount of respect and honor. Try to slow down when praying the Hail Mary from now on.

Lesson 12

A New Way to Pray

St. Ignatius of Loyola

We spend our entire lives praying to God. We pray to Him in the morning and evening, before meals and maybe after meals, when we go to church, and occasionally throughout the day. For some believers, their prayer life might be fairly simple. They pray their scripted prayers like the Our Father or Hail Mary. They might have the assistance of a prayer book and read their prayers. When I was studying to be a priest, I went through a program called the Institute for Priestly Formation. The summer began with an eight-day silent retreat, which was meant to teach us how to pray like St. Ignatius of Loyola.

It was a new way of praying for me. I had been trained in the Benedictine tradition at Conception Seminary, so one way I learned to pray was through *lectio divina*, or holy reading. This is when you read a passage of Scripture and pray with a word or phrase that spoke to you in your prayerful reading. Then you would dialogue with the Lord about it. Ignatian prayer was similar yet different. It was personal and relational. You were to pray with your senses. It involved the use of the imagination and placing yourself in the biblical scene. You would consider what you saw or heard, maybe even what you smelled. This prayerful engagement with Scripture would lead a person to a colloquy or prayerful consideration with the Trinity, Mary, or the saints.

The brilliance of Ignatian spirituality is even more extraordinary given that St. Ignatius was not always a holy man. Growing up in a castle in Loyola with his brother, Martin, and Martin's wife, Magdalena, Ignatius was surrounded by holy images. When Martin and Madgalena married, Queen Isabella gifted the couple a painting of the Annunciation, which was housed in the castle's new chapel. There were other statues of Our Lady, including Our Lady of Sorrows and Our Lady of Olatz.

Ignatius left the family castle and joined the military. He lived a debauched, secular life, pursuing carnal desires. An unfortunate accident with a cannonball left Ignatius bedridden for months. To pass the time he asked for some books to read. While he wanted some secular reading, he was instead given *The Life of Jesus Christ* by Ludolph of Saxony and *The Golden Legend: Lives of the Saints* by Jacobus de Voragine. His heart, which searched for love in all the wrong ways, now encountered the story of a God of love and those who loved that God. These books marked the beginning of his conversion. As a way to thank Our Lady for obtaining the grace of his recovery and consequent conversion, Ignatius spent the entirety of one night at a shrine of Our Lady. This is something that he would repeat again at the Shrine of Our Lady of Montserrat.

Ignatius founded the Jesuit order and his Spiritual Exercises would become the basis of spiritual formation for the men who joined. While many people might undergo a modified form of the Spiritual Exercises, like three days or eight days, Ignatius envisioned the process as a thirty-day retreat, based on four weeks. The second week focuses on the Incarnation—that is, God becoming man and being born of Mary. Naturally, one would be drawn to pray and reflect on Mary. Ignatius encourages the retreatant: "Conceive, then, a great respect and confidence for the Mother of God, and never forget that the Word incarnate having only come into the world through Mary, it is only by Mary that we can go to Him."[43] In another meditation he encourages the reader to imagine being at the manger with Jesus, Mary, and Joseph. Not only does he encourage one to imagine these scenes, he invites the individual to go make a colloquy or have a conversation with Mary or Jesus about the events.

In one sentence of the Spiritual Exercises, St. Ignatius urges us to reflect on the baptism of Jesus, which marks the beginning of His public ministry. Ignatius writes, "Jesus having bid adieu to His Mother set out from Nazareth, and went to the banks of the river Jordan, where John, His precursor, was baptizing."[44] Just as a parent has to say goodbye to their child when leaving them at college, Mary had to accept Jesus leaving home to begin His mission of preaching. Ignatius invites us to pause and call to mind that image. What took place? Did the mother and son embrace? Did Mary shed a tear in that moment? We know that it would only be a short while until the wedding in Cana, which was an early moment in Jesus' ministry and the beginning of his public miracles. This would have been another time when Mary would have had to say goodbye to Jesus again for a time. This leads into another possible meditation about Mary's approaching Jesus, as is the case in Mark 3:31–35, and whether Mary would have been present as a follower at other moments of Jesus' ministry.

In the fourth week, Ignatius invites us to meditate on Christ's Resurrection. Each year we hear the account of Christ's Resurrection

---

[43] Ignatius of Loyola, *The Spiritual Exercises of Saint Ignatius: or Manresa* (Charlotte: TAN Classics, 1999), 105.

[44] Ignatius, *Spiritual Exercises*, 269.

on Easter Sunday. We know that Mary Magdalene was at the tomb and that Jesus appeared to her. She announced to the apostles that the tomb was empty. Peter and John ran to the tomb and confirmed what Mary Magdalene said. The Scripture tells us that Mary Magdalene was the first to see Jesus. But Ignatius and many others have offered an alternative possibility—namely, that Jesus appeared to His mother, Mary, in a meeting that is not recorded in Scripture. Ignatius believed He would have done this because of Mary's participation and sharing in Christ's Passion. This then becomes a point for personal prayer. Imagine what took place in that meeting: what Mary saw, how Jesus addressed her, what other words they exchanged, how they said goodbye once more. In the colloquy, Ignatius encourages a person to congratulate Mary on her happiness and to rejoice with her that Christ is risen from the dead.[45]

St. Ignatius was surrounded by the Blessed Mother from a young age, and as she does for so many, she brought him back to the fold when he went astray. He spent time in prayer at her shrines and entrusted the Jesuit order to her intercession under the title Madonna della Strada. In his method of prayer, he teaches us new ways to pray about the person of Mary and encourages us to converse with her as our mother. His example teaches us new ways to pray and engage with Mary in our personal prayer.

How to Love Mary Like St. Ignatius

- Make some time to visit a shrine of Our Lady. You probably won't be able to spend an entire night there, but spend a morning or afternoon in prayer.

[45] Ignatius, *Spiritual Exercises*, 172.

- Pray the Rosary using your imagination. This might be the easiest way to integrate this style of prayer into your life. Pray with the Nativity, or Jesus's ministry, or His Resurrection appearance to Mary.
- Talk to Mary about anything going on in your life. Go to her for motherly counsel and advice.

Lesson 13

He Preached the Virgin Mother's Glory

St. Bernard of Clairvaux

After graduating from Conception Seminary, I studied at Mundelein Seminary in the suburbs of Chicago. One of the first research papers I wrote was for a class on medieval Church history. I cannot recall why, but I chose to write on the Marian homilies of St. Bernard of Clairvaux, a Cistercian monk who served as abbot at the monastery of Clairvaux. As a budding Marian theologian, I probably selected him because on his feast day the Church's antiphon in evening prayer called him a preeminent preacher of the Virgin Mother's glory. His homilies are read as part of the Office of Readings throughout the liturgical year.

After encountering the Marian sermons of St. Bernard of Clairvaux early on in my theological study, I decided that my licentiate thesis would focus on the Assumption sermons of St. Bernard. The thought and preaching of St. Bernard have tremendously impacted my own priestly life and preaching.

St. Bernard of Clairvaux was born in 1090 and died in 1153. His spiritual influence was felt within the Church as he wrote to the popes and in political life as he advised rulers. He was fascinated with the Song of Songs from the Old Testament. His sermons on that book are published in four English volumes. He wrote several spiritual treatises, including *On Loving God, On Conversion, On the Steps of Humility and Pride,* and *On Consideration.* As an abbot, it was his responsibility to preach to the monastery on principal feast days throughout the year. His sermons on these feasts are also published in several volumes and are available for one's spiritual reading. It is these homilies that show the richness of St. Bernard's prayer life, the fruit of his *lectio divina,* and the magnificence of his preaching. When we hear preachers today break open the Word of God, sometimes something they say can remain with us for the rest of our lives. Their sound bite is forever remembered. This is the case with St. Bernard of Clairvaux. Once you encounter his reflections, you will call them to mind again and again. At least, that's the case for me.

Each Advent, we anticipate the birth of Jesus. This anticipation was realized in Mary when she received the announcement of Jesus' birth from the angel Gabriel. In a sense, the whole world anticipated this moment because our history would be redeemed. The original sin of Adam and Eve would be righted. Most believed the Messiah would come as a military leader or political figure, but God intended to send Him as a little baby and for Him to be an itinerant preacher and healer. St. Bernard of Clairvaux, in his homily *Super Missus Est* (sometimes known in English as *In Praise of the Virgin Mary*), captures the scene in his beautiful writing:

> You have heard, O Virgin, that you will conceive and bear a son; you have heard that it will not be by man but by the Holy Spirit. The angel awaits an answer; it is time for him to return to God who sent him. We too are waiting, O Lady, for your word of compassion; the sentence of

condemnation weighs heavily upon us.... Tearful Adam with his sorrowing family begs this of you, O loving Virgin, in their exile from Paradise. Abraham begs it, David begs it. All the other holy patriarchs, your ancestors, ask it of you, as they dwell in the country of the shadow of death.... Answer quickly, O Virgin. Reply in haste to the angel, or rather through the angel of the Lord. Answer with a word, receive the Word of God. Speak your own word, conceive the divine Word. Breathe a passing word, embrace the eternal Word.[46]

And as the whole world waits, Mary gives her answer: "Behold I am the handmaid of the Lord." This preaching of St. Bernard is so rich as he captures the collective waiting for the Redeemer. With his descriptive words, it's almost as if we can see this happening. And as Mary gives her fiat, we can see the relief and joy of all those awaiting redemption and the angels, for the savior is going to be born.

In the same homily, St. Bernard addresses our relationship to Mary and how she can help us during the storms of life. He encourages us to invoke the name of Mary, for she will assist her children.

She, I say, is that shining and brilliant star, so much needed, set in place above life's great and spacious sea, glittering with merits, all aglow with examples for our imitation. Oh, whosoever thou art that perceiveth thyself during this mortal existence to be rather drifting in treacherous waters, at the mercy of the winds and the waves, than walking on firm ground, turn not away thine eyes from the splendor of this guiding star, unless thou

[46] *Liturgy of the Hours,* vol. 1, 345.

wish to be submerged by the storm! When the storms to temptation burst upon thee, when thou seest thyself driven upon the rocks of tribulation, look at the star, call upon Mary. When buffeted by the billows of pride, or ambition, or hatred, or jealousy, look at the star, call upon Mary. Should anger, or avarice, or fleshly desire violently assail the frail vessel of thy soul, look at the star, call upon Mary. If troubled on account of the heinousness of thy sins, distressed at the filthy state of thy conscience, and terrified at the thought of the awful judgment to come, thou art beginning to sink into the bottomless gulf of sadness and to be swallowed in the abyss of despair, then think of Mary. In dangers, in doubts, in difficulties, think of Mary, call upon Mary. Let not her name leave thy lips, never suffer it to leave thy heart. And that thou mayest more surely obtain the assistance of her prayer, see that thou dost walk in her footsteps. With her for guide, thou shalt never go astray; whilst invoking her, thou shalt never lose heart; so long as she is in thy mind, thou shalt not be deceived; whilst she holds thy hand, thou canst not fall; under her protection, thou hast nothing to fear; if she walks before thee, thou shalt not grow weary; if she shows thee favor, thou shalt reach the goal.[47]

Mary is the star of the sea; she will guide us. We are the voyager, and our destination is eternity. Mary, as the star, will guide us to our heavenly port. St. Bernard must have found Mary to be an excellent intercessor in his life because what he encouraged,

---

[47] Translation from Pope Pius XII's encyclical *Doctor Mellifluus*, paragraph 31.

he must have known and experienced himself. When vices like pride or jealousy confronted him, he turned to Mary's intercession. At the lowest moments of our life, when all hope is lost, we find hope in the motherly intercession of Mary. Just as a mother attends to her child, so does our heavenly mother. When you face a difficulty in your life, don't be afraid to turn to Mary and call upon her name for help.

Mary can be our helper in our time of need because God has allowed her to be our mediatrix of grace. St. Bernard, in his homily "On the Nativity of Blessed Mary," captures this beautifully as he describes Mary to be an overflowing aqueduct: "Truly that aqueduct is full so that others may take of its fullness, but not the full measure itself."[48] God has chosen Mary to be our mediatrix of grace. He bestowed that office upon her. She who was so full of grace now can allow that grace to overflow to us. Bernard had great confidence in the mediation of Mary because he experienced it himself.

Another way that Bernard's preaching has enriched my prayer and meditation is through his sermons on the Assumption. One point he draws out which can enliven our prayer is the welcome of Mary in Heaven. He offers these words: "How great do you think was the joy of the citizens of heaven when they succeeded in hearing her voice, seeing her face, and enjoying her blessed presence."[49] When you have prayed about the Assumption and celebrated the solemnity as a holy day of obligation, did you ever consider the reception of Mary into eternity? Such a simple sentence from

---

[48] St. Bernard of Clairvaux, *Sermons for the Autumn Season*, "On the Nativity of Blessed Mary," paragraph 3, 72.

[49] St. Bernard, *Sermons for the Autumn Season*, "Of the Double Assumption," paragraph 1, 14.

Bernard can have us meditating upon the joy of the angels and saints as she entered the heavenly kingdom.

One of Bernard's most popular writings is *On Loving God*. In this spiritual work, he breaks down four degrees by which a person can have love for God. The first degree is when man loves himself for his own sake. The second is when man loves God for his own good. The third is loving God for God's sake, and the fourth, loving himself for the sake of God. The first love is a more self-centered love, not focusing on neighbor or God. The second is a love of God because God can do something for the person. The third is loving God for who He is. The fourth is a pure love: the person loves God because of who God made him to be and what God has done for him.

I believe that we can take these degrees of loving God and examine our love for the Mother of God in a similar way. Ask yourself: Why do I love Mary? Someone might love Mary because they have asked her prayers often and received the graces by the means of her intercession and mediation of grace. That is loving Mary because she can do something for us. Instead, we should foster a love of Mary for who she was and is still today in eternity. We love Mary because she gave birth to the Savior of the world and facilitated the means of our salvation and redemption. We love Mary because Jesus gave her to us as a mother at the foot of the Cross. We love Mary because she lived a life like ours and has preceded us in eternity, and in how she lived her life we find a virtuous example to imitate.

St. Bernard loved the Blessed Mother. He has earned the title of Troubadour of Mary and the Marian doctor for his beautiful writings on Mary. Among the preachers, he is an eminent preacher of her glory. His preaching aids us in meditation and appreciating who Mary was in the history of salvation.

How to Love Mary Like St. Bernard of Clairvaux

• Use his preaching to enrich your prayer and meditation. Pray about Mary giving her yes to the angel or about her reception in the heavenly courts.

• Have you experienced the help of Mary in a troubling time? Give thanks to God for her intercession. Next time when you face a troubling situation or temptation, hear the voice of St. Bernard and call out to Mary.

• Think about the reasons why you love Mary and, if you can, purify those reasons.

Lesson 14

Mary Is Our Lifelong Friend

Francis Cardinal George, OMI

A northern suburb of Chicago was my home for four years as I studied for the priesthood at Mundelein Seminary. I had a few occasions to visit the city itself and enjoy many of its Catholic scenes. During my time at Mundelein, for three of the four years, Francis Cardinal George was still serving as archbishop. I spoke with him only a few times, perhaps because I was too timid, though I had the occasion to serve as a deacon at a Mass he celebrated.

Francis Cardinal George (1937–2015) was an intellectual giant of the Catholic Church and served as the president of the United States Conference of Catholic Bishops from 2007 to 2010. Ordained to the priesthood in 1963, he was named bishop of Yakima, Washington, in 1990 and then as archbishop of Portland, Oregon, before being named the archbishop of Chicago in 1997 — a post he served in until his retirement in 2014, followed by a cancer diagnosis that ultimately would claim his life. If there is anything apparent in the life of Cardinal George, it is the Marian devotion that remained a constant all through his life, even to the last moments of life. For him Mary was a lifelong friend, mother, companion, and intercessor.

How They Love Mary

According to his priest secretary of nearly twenty years, Fr. Daniel Flens, "Cardinal George did not wear his love for the Blessed Mother 'on his sleeve,' but it had to be instilled in him as a child and deepened and focused after he entered the Missionary Oblates of Mary Immaculate." Cardinal George's sister, Margaret Cain, recalled a few memories of her brother and his Marian devotion. In every room of their house there was an image of Mary. On the dressers, a statue. In their living room, there hung a picture of the Holy Family that Cardinal George painted. They would gather together in May and crown the statue of Our Lady, sing her hymns, and offer her flowers. On the occasion of his First Holy Communion on May 5, 1945, Cardinal George was enrolled in the brown scapular, technically known as the Confraternity of the Scapular of Our Lady of Mount Carmel: a sacramental worn out of devotion to Mary and a request for her protection at one's hour of death. The scapular is typically made of brown cloth, but some people wear a scapular medal, which according to Cardinal George replaced the cloth "for convenience's sake."

From a young age, Francis George also had a desire toward the priesthood. God was already at work in his life from a very young age, and the seed of his vocation began to germinate on the occasion of his First Communion. As a native Chicagoan, George entered the high school seminary at Quigley. But due to health complications from polio and his use of crutches, he was unable to navigate the public transportation system, forcing him to seek out a boarding school instead. He enrolled in a high school seminary in Belleville, Illinois, where he was introduced for the first time to the Oblates of Mary Immaculate. Cardinal George made his solemn profession of vows with the Missionary Oblates on September 8, 1961, the feast of Mary's Nativity, and was ordained a priest on December 21, 1963, just in time for him to celebrate his first Christmas as a priest. He rose to the rank of vicar general of the Oblates and oversaw the editing of the order's prayer book. Contained in the prayer book is the seventeenth-century French School of Spirituality prayer from Jacques Olier, "Jesus living in Mary, come and live in your servants." This prayer was one recited every morning by the cardinal at the end of the time he set aside for meditation. In his words, "It expresses who we are, united to Christ in Mary, and how we are expected to transform our lives day by day."

The Oblate General House in Rome was home to Cardinal George for fourteen years and was home to him whenever he visited Rome. His priest secretary recalled many of their visits together. Upon arriving at the Generalate, the prayerful cardinal would enter the house chapel, pray before the Blessed Sacrament, and then greet the Oblate Madonna housed in the chapel. The statue has a storied history within the order because it was associated with St. Eugene de Mazenod, the founder of the Oblates, who had a mystical experience with it. The miraculous statue of the Oblate Madonna came to life: the Virgin opened her eyes, nodded her head, and smiled at the founder. Throughout his life, St. Eugene de Mazenod would return to pray before the statue many times, asking for extraordinary graces. Just like the founder of his congregation, Cardinal George returned many times to pray before an image of Mary so revered by his religious community and its venerable founder.

Cardinal George was a lifelong devotee of the Rosary. He would quietly pray it by himself but, being a leader of prayer, he would also lead pilgrims to Mary's shrines in this prayer and at times would be asked by various apostolates to lead a Rosary recording that would be used by the faithful for their personal prayer. In his writings, he described the Rosary as a key form of intercession and recommended that individuals pray it for specific intentions. During the month of October—the month of the Holy Rosary, and also Respect for Life Month—Cardinal George encouraged, in a 2009 article, the recitation of the Rosary for children threatened with abortion and for their mothers and fathers. He also encouraged praying the Rosary for the healing of victims of clergy sexual abuse. He said, "The rosary is a powerful prayer because it helps us identify our lives with those of the Lord and his Blessed Mother. We insert what happens to us into what happened to them."

Cardinal George was also a pilgrim and a leader of pilgrimages. In 2011, on the occasion of World Youth Day in Madrid, Cardinal George made a visit to the site of the famed 1917 apparitions of Our Lady in Fatima, Portugal. For devotees of the Rosary, Fatima plays an important role in that devotion, not only because Our Lady requested its daily recitation for peace in the world, but also because Mary taught the children a new prayer to be prayed after each decade, "O my Jesus ... "

As archbishop of Chicago, Cardinal George wrote a weekly column for the diocesan newspaper. With the unsettling news of clergy sexual abuse and cover-up, Cardinal George saw the message of Fatima as pertinent to healing the Church, stating that we needed to make "constant atonement, reconciliation, and reparation." He cited the example of the saints who took on penance for the sins of others and desired to repair the wounds of the Church and the world.

As Our Lady asked for the Rosary to be prayed for peace in the world, Cardinal George asked the faithful of Chicago to pray the Rosary for victims of sexual abuse. It seems a fitting request that complements the Fatima message, asking for God to bestow peace in their hearts and souls, and also to restore peace in the Church.

Cardinal George was also a pilgrim. A favorite destination was Lourdes in France. One of the popular aspects of a Lourdes pilgrimage is bathing in the healing waters, a prayerful ritual that requires the help of volunteers to lower individuals into the water. As the sick (*malades*) would wait to enter the water, a fellow pilgrim named Peter Scudner recalled, Cardinal George would pray with them and visit with them. A pilgrimage to Lourdes for the cardinal was a unique experience because he was both a leader and a *malade*. He suffered the effects of polio from childhood, and even when pain would overcome him, he would not allow it to halt his ministry to the sick in Lourdes. And he battled cancer in later years. There in the waters of Lourdes, he prayed for the grace of healing—not only for himself, but for Mary's beloved children who are suffering around the world.

On the feast of the Assumption in 2012, Cardinal George was given an opportunity to pray and contemplate his own mortality as he faced his cancer diagnosis. In 2015, as his hour of death drew nearer, the cardinal made a simple request; he wanted those present to pray the Rosary, which is exactly what they did. Margaret Cain, Cardinal George's sister, recalled that the Salve Regina, or Hail, Holy Queen, was chanted in Latin. The words seem quite appropriate on the occasion of someone's death. It speaks of us sighing, mourning, and weeping. As a dedicated priest son of Mary Immaculate, no doubt God heard and answered those prayers recited and sung at his deathbed. Mary did truly pray for him at the hour of his death.

How to Love Mary Like Francis Cardinal George

- Wear the brown scapular. If you are a parent or grandparent, see to it that the little ones in your life are enrolled.
- Bring flowers to Mary at your local parish. They could be flowers from your garden or flowers you bought.

- Pray the Rosary and do so for prayer intentions. You may wish to dedicate an entire Rosary to an intention, maybe a decade for an intention, or even call to mind an intention for each bead.
- Do something special for Mary during the month of May.
- Pray the Memorare.
- Make an occasional visit to a statue of Mary at your parish church or wherever it might be located. Is there a statue that has been passed down for generations or has special meaning for you?
- Look up a musical version of the Salve Regina and listen to the beautiful chant. Pray the Hail, Holy Queen or learn the words to it in Latin.
- You might not be able to visit Lourdes, France, but at churches, retreat centers, and shrines throughout the world, grotto replicas may be found. Seek out the nearest Lourdes grotto, visit, and pray, asking Mary to pray for those you know who are sick.

Lesson 15

The Goodness of Devotion to Mary

Blessed Columba Marmion

One of the spiritual formators at Mundelein Seminary was a retired abbot from Marmion Abbey in Aurora, Illinois. The monastery of monks also sent their monks in training to be priests to the seminary as well. This began my familiarity with a monk spiritual writer named Blessed Columba Marmion. Another one of my professors, a diocesan priest who would later join Marmion Abbey, held Columba Marmion in high esteem and wanted us to be exposed to his writings, making Marmion required reading for the class.

Then there was a research trip to Belgium. I knew I would need places to stay during my trip, and it just so happened that the abbey of Maredsous, where Marmion served as abbot, was near one of my destinations. They had a guest house where I stayed, and it offered me the opportunity to pray at the grave of Marmion — not only for my own priesthood but for all those I knew who were devoted to him.

Columba Marmion was born Joseph Marmion on April 1, 1858, in Dublin. His father was French and his mother was Irish. He was raised in a religious household and received a good Catholic education. He decided to study for the diocesan priesthood and took up studies at Holy Cross College before studying in Rome. He was ordained a priest in 1881. During his studies for the priesthood, he began to sense the monastic call. The first instance of this calling came during a visit to Monte Cassino. While participating in the monastic life there, Marmion wished to remain there instead of returning to Rome. After his priestly ordination, he visited Maredsous Abbey for the first time to see a friend who had joined the monastery. Again, he strongly desired to remain at Maredsous but felt he must return to Dublin and serve the local church.

In 1886, five years after priestly ordination, Marmion chose to test his monastic vocation and joined Maredsous. He gained a reputation as an outstanding preacher. Catholics traveled from all parts of Ireland to hear him preach. He was elected abbot of Maredsous in 1909 and died in 1923.

In *Christ, the Life of the Soul*, Marmion offers an intimate spiritual portrait of Our Lord, often through the eyes of His Blessed Mother. Marmion writes: "A soul's loving devotion would not be truly Christian if it did not include within its object the mother of the Incarnate Word. Devotion towards the Virgin Mary is not only important but necessary if we wish to draw abundantly from the source of life."[50]

Furthermore, when we talk about Mary and her privileges, we are giving praise to God. Marmion says: "Jesus loved His mother by—as God—showering sublime privileges upon her. And we, we shall show our love by extolling those privileges."[51] As we see what God has done in and through Mary as Mother of the Redeemer, we are moved to give thanks to the Trinity and imitate Jesus in His

---

[50] Columba Marmion, *Christ, the Life of the Soul* (Bethesda, MD: Zaccheus Press, 2005), 470.
[51] Marmion, *Christ, the Life of the Soul*, 481.

thoughts and love. And the way we give our thanks and demonstrate this is through the many devotions to Mary in the Church.

Blessed Columba Marmion's devotion to Mary was enriched by his personal prayer and meditation, as well as the liturgy. While often remaining at the abbey, Marmion did make a pilgrimage to the Marian shrine in Lourdes, France. The pilgrimage made an impression on him, and while there he preached, "My heart is overjoyed to see this great witness of filial love of her children towards Mary."[52]

Marmion's approach to Marian devotion was balanced. It's easy for us to be overwhelmed by the sheer variety of devotions approved by the Church. As you've no doubt realized by now, one cannot perform them all! But, as Marmion assures us, that's okay. "It is not necessary to weigh oneself down with 'practices,'" he wrote. "One should choose some; but stay faithful to what has been chosen once the choice has been made. Such daily homage given to His mother will be one that could not be more pleasing to our Lord."[53]

What are some of the practices of Marian piety that he recommends? First is the Rosary. He says it's "an excellent 'practice' to recite the rosary every day with devotion."[54] By doing so, we draw close to Christ in His mysteries, and in our greeting to Mary and our petition of her, we obtain graces for the present moment and also at the hour of our death. The Rosary is also a means by which "we render to the Saviour, by the mediation of Mary, the worship of our thought and of our love, in His childhood, in His suffering

[52] Rev. David Hankus, *Blessed Columba Marmion and His Understanding of the Role of the Blessed Virgin Mary in the Life of a Roman Catholic Priest* (n.p.: Xlibris, 2013), 19.
[53] Marmion, *Christ, the Life of the Soul*, 484.
[54] Marmion, *Christ, the Life of the Soul*, 483.

95

and in His glory, and in virtue of this contact of faith many divine aids are accorded to us," including the virtues presented in the mysteries.[55]

In addition to the Rosary, he recommends Mary's seasonal antiphons, which are sung as part of compline (or night prayer). He also urges us to observe the Angelus and recite Mary's litanies.[56]

Marmion also makes specific suggestions for priests. He urges us to entrust the souls of hardened sinners to Our Lady.[57] He encourages priests to rely on the Blessed Virgin Mary's prayerful support, so that we may celebrate the Mass well.[58] He recommends that, after Mass, a priest should renew his devotion to Mary.[59]

Of course, this advice has relevance for the laity too. Any lay-man can ask Mary to help them be attentive during Mass—and they should! We should formulate these intentions in the moments before Mass, as we prepare in the church. Mary can also be a subject of our prayer and thoughts following Mass as we realize that just like her, we now have the living God inside of us through Holy Communion.

A simple but powerful devotion is to say the Hail Mary very slowly, with great sincerity and intentionality.[60] Finally, he recommends that we "at all times pay to Our Lady the tribute of our filial thoughts"[61] and place ourselves under her protection.[62] These

---

[55] Columba Marmion, *Christ: The Ideal of the Priest* (San Francisco: Ignatius Press, 2005), 341.
[56] Marmion, *Christ, the Life of the Soul*, 483.
[57] Marmion, *Christ: The Ideal of the Priest*, 339.
[58] Marmion, *Christ: The Ideal of the Priest*, 343.
[59] Marmion, *Christ: The Ideal of the Priest*, 340.
[60] Marmion, *Christ: The Ideal of the Priest*, 340.
[61] Marmion, *Christ: The Ideal of the Priest*, 344.
[62] Marmion, *Christ: The Ideal of the Priest*, 345.

recommendations of Marmion certainly deepen our love for the Blessed Mother because he wants us to better the devotion we already possess.

Columba Marmion realized that Marian devotion pleased Jesus and that it was good for the devotee. By it, we live in imitation of Jesus and through it we receive the necessary graces for our Christian life. He concludes his chapter in *Christ, the Life of the Soul* with a few simple petitions to Our Lady, asking her for faith and for the graces we need to live our life. If we want to honor Our Lady the most, we should do so by loving and honoring her Son: "The Virgin Mary has no greater wish than to see her Divine Son obeyed, loved, glorified, exalted."[63] Love Mary because Jesus wants you to. Love Jesus because Mary wants you to.

How to Love Mary Like Blessed Columba Marmion

* Reflect on your reasons for loving Mary.
* Do you feel overwhelmed by the amount of Marian devotions possible? Which do you feel most drawn to? Which have been most effective in drawing you closer to Our Lord through Our Lady? Are there new ones you want to try?
* When you next attend Mass, ask for her help in remaining attentive throughout.
* Pray the Hail Mary slowly and reverently, meditating on the meaning of these familiar words.

---

[63] Marmion, *Christ, the Life of the Soul*, 491.

Lesson 16

A Life of Union with Jesus and Mary

Fr. Emile Neubert

I once received a message from a brother priest I had never met but who followed me on social media. He told me that he was interested in incorporating Mary more into his priestly ministry and asked for a recommendation. I recommended Fr. Emile Neubert's *Mary and the Priestly Ministry*. It just so happened that I met this priest a few months later when I was on a pilgrimage within his diocese, and he shared with me how he picked up the book and it was tremendously helpful in his spiritual life and priestly ministry.

Johnnette Benkovic Williams, host of *Women of Grace* on EWTN, also found Fr. Neubert to be inspirational. I've been a guest on her show a few times, and during a break she asked me if I knew anything about Fr. Neubert. I told her that I really liked his writings and recommended them to others. A few months went by, and I received an invitation from her to lead a retreat for her Women of Grace leaders based on the writings and spirituality of Fr. Neubert. She had read his *Queen of Militants*, a handbook on Christian life and living as a disciple of Jesus and Mary, and was blown away.

Emile Neubert was born during Mary's month on May 8, 1878. He joined a religious community dedicated to the Blessed

Virgin, the Marianists, founded by Bl. William Chaminade in 1892. He was ordained a priest in 1906. Before delving deeper into the writings of Fr. Neubert, it is important to understand the influences on his spiritual life. He was profoundly impacted by the French School of Spirituality, a movement inspired by writers like Cardinal Bérulle, St. John Eudes, Jean-Jacques Olier, and St. Louis de Montfort. One of the emphases of the French School was the Incarnation, that God became like us and took flesh from Mary. Other aspects of the movement focused on the Hearts of Jesus and Mary, the spiritual life of Jesus and Mary, and consecration to Jesus — first promoted by Bérulle and developed by de Montfort.

Biographers of Fr. Emile gave him the nickname "Our Lady's Dolphin." Just as other animals have significance in Christianity (like the pelican, who pecks her breast to feed her babies, just as Christ feeds us in the Eucharist), the dolphin symbolizes diligence, love, and swiftness. Fr. Emile was a dolphin for Mary. If you have watched a dolphin eat, they can be voracious; Fr. Emile was voracious in his zeal for souls.

Fr. Emile went to great ends to preach the faith. A dolphin can render its prey immobile; Fr. Emile did this with his arguments for Christianity. A dolphin has a built-in smile; Fr. Emile was a joyful man. He was a very learned man, especially when it came to the Blessed Virgin Mary. He could rightly be considered one of the greatest Mariologists of the twentieth century.

Though an accomplished scholar, he had a childlike love for the Blessed Mother as well. He came to the United States and upon arrival commented: "I landed in New York and as I walked about, I thought to myself, what a wonderful land, look how they have numbered their streets in honor of the Blessed Mother's rosary: First Avenue, Second Avenue, Third Avenue." His academic career and ministry led him to become the rector of the seminary in Fribourg. He died in 1967.

In his preaching and writing, he wanted to communicate love for Mary in imitation of Jesus. Perhaps his best-known work is *My Ideal: Jesus, Son of Mary*. In it, Fr. Emile says that we should give ourselves to her without reserve, that we should love, obey, honor, and resemble her, have confidence in her, be united with her, and listen to her. Not only does he present that we should imitate Jesus in our love of Mary, but he instructs us with the voice of Mary, who wants us to become like Jesus. His book *Life of Union with Mary* provides an in-depth look at how we live united with Mary.

For instance, he recommends that we seek to love Mary with the heart of Jesus and to love Jesus with the heart of Mary. It is in a union with these two hearts that we love the other. The union we strive after is union of thought, will, sentiments, general activity, spiritual exercises, spiritual work, and practice of the virtues. We can be united with Mary as we reflect on the life of Jesus or receive it in Holy Communion. When we suffer, we can be united with Mary as she stood at the foot of the Cross. We can be united with Mary in our daily activity. When I wash my clothes or cook a meal, I can think of Mary, who did these very things in her own life. If we strive to live a life in union with Mary, we will do our best to please God.

Fr. Emile's book *Mary's Apostolic Mission and Ours* had a profound impact on me. When I read it, I had already done a lot of writing and research about the Marian apparition in Champion, Wisconsin, where Mary asked us to pray for the conversion of sinners. The main premise behind this book is the need to cooperate with Mary in obtaining the salvation of souls. In it, Fr. Emile says: "Mary's mission is to snatch souls from Satan so that she might make of God's enemies who are ready to fall into hell, his friends, his well-beloved children, who will praise him eternally in Heaven.... But since he has need of us, Mary cannot achieve these results without our help."[64]

Fr. Emile sought to form Christian men and women according to their station in life. He wrote to priests in *Mary and the Priestly Ministry*, showing how Mary aids them in their priestly life giving them an example and model, knowing of their prayers, and explaining how they can exercise their ministry in union with Mary. He wrote to families in his book *Mary and the Christian Family* and to educators in *Mary and the Christian Educator*.

The most comprehensive formation manual that Fr. Emile wrote was *Queen of Militants*, which shows how Mary is raising up the next generation of saints. He explains how she will keep you in the friendship of Christ and teach you true love for men. She will give you the soul of the apostolate. She will teach you courage, perseverance, and self-forgetfulness. She will console you. She will transform you into another Christ.

Fr. Emile also gave the following advice to those struggling with impurity, advice that has become popular with confessors around the world: "Each morning upon rising say the Hail Mary three times, with the invocation, 'O Mary, conceived without sin, pray for us who have recourse to thee,' asking our Blessed Mother to keep us pure throughout the day. Do the same in the evening when you retire so that she will preserve us from all sin during the night."[65] He encourages us to carry a miraculous medal and a rosary on our person at all times. He also encourages Marian

---

[64] Fr. Emile Neubert, *Mary's Apostolic Mission and Ours* (New Bedford, MA: Academy of the Immaculate, 2011), 288–289.
[65] Fr. Emile Neubert, *Queen of Militants* (St. Meinrad, IN: Grail Publications, 1947), 55.

consecration, but even more than the act of consecration, he urges us to *live* our consecration intentionally each day.[66] He also believed in efficacious invocations: short little prayers addressed to Mary, which he modeled in writings.

Fr. Emile loved Our Lady. He wanted all people to grow in their love for her as a means of imitating Jesus. And Jesus wants us to be aware of her apostolic mission and make it ours. He taught me to live my life in union with Mary—and how, by doing so, I can assist her in snatching souls from the devil.

How to Love Mary Like Fr. Emile Neubert

• Ask yourself what are ways you can become aware of living your life in union with Mary right now? How can Mary encourage you in your state of life?
• Begin and end your day with three Hail Marys.
• Formulate a short prayer that you can pray throughout the day. It could be as simple as "Mary, help me."

[66] Neubert, *Queen of Militants*, 47–50; Fr. Emile Neubert, *Life of Union with Mary* (Milwaukee: Bruce, 1959), 14–18.

Lesson 17

The Realness and Relatability of Mary

Caryll Houselander

One day, I was listening to a guest lecturer from Chicago speak on Marian spirituality. My mentor had studied under this man and had a great deal of respect for him. During the lecture he said, "My favorite book about Mary is *The Reed of God* by Caryll Houselander." While discussing the lecture with some friends afterward, I think I scoffed at the book. I'd heard of it, though I hadn't read it. A few years ago, I received a gratis copy of *The Reed of God*. Since it was given to me by the publisher, I felt obliged to read it.

I understood why it was considered a spiritual classic.

Caryll Houselander was a laywoman. Born in 1901 in England, her family life was quite broken, and her parents divorced when she was nine years old. Even then, it was clear that she was gifted, but (as is so often the case with talented young people) she didn't fit in well with the crowd. She was an artist and poet who was touched by God's grace, becoming a mystic and a popular spiritual writer.

Curiously, Houselander was a Catholic convert. Her family was Anglican but, at the age of six, Caryll's mother, Gertrude, converted to Catholicism. Caryll didn't appreciate the gift of her faith and sought faith in other Christian denominations and world religions like Buddhism, before settling into the Russian Orthodox Church for some time. She fell in love with a Russian spy who broke her heart. Eventually, she returned home to Catholicism and fostered a deep, mystical prayer life.

Houselander gained a reputation for her holiness, and many sought her religious counsel as a spiritual director. Her Marian classic, *The Reed of God*, appeared in 1944 and, in 1954, she died of breast cancer.

Advent was a dominant theme in Houselander's writings. For Our Lady, she explains, there were several advents. There was the advent of her waiting with all of Israel for the coming of the Messiah, which was a type of pre-advent in her virginal waiting. There was the advent of her pregnancy, waiting to adore the face of God to come forth from her womb. After the death of the Lord, Mary entered another advent of her life as she awaited her reunion with Him. Now, Houselander writes, "she had come to another Advent, a preparation for seeing her Son's face in heaven, and it was to be lived out in exactly the same way."[67]

These seasons of Advent, when lived in imitation of Our Lady, allow us to grow in many ways, especially of love and silence. But just as Mary allowed Christ to grow within her, Houselander says that during our Advent season we must allow Christ to grow in us. During Mary's Advent, she brought Christ into the world; we must also bring Christ to others, as she did. Just as Mary waited to see Christ, we wait to see Christ each time in the Eucharist and at our end in Heaven.

Houselander also devotes a great deal of attention to the loss of Jesus in the Temple and Mary's seeking to find Him. Those who

---

[67] Caryll Houselander, *The Reed of God* (Notre Dame, IN: Ave Maria Press, 2020), 169.

pray the Rosary will know this event as the fifth Joyful Mystery, which focuses more on the positive—the finding of Jesus. But it is also one of the seven sorrows of Mary, when she seeks Jesus and cannot find him for three days. Like us, Mary knows what it means to lose something—someone—we love. She suffered the loss of her son; in the same instant, she also suffered the loss of God.

As Christians, we experience the loss of Christ especially through our sins. For Houselander, Mary—though sinless—teaches us how to seek out Jesus and to find Him once again.

Houselander also emphasizes Mary's relationship to the human race. She had a keen understanding of the teaching of the Mystical Body of Christ that St. Paul writes about, and which was unpacked in the 1943 magisterial document of Pius XII *Mystici Corporis Christi*. Houselander says, "In giving her humanity to God, Mary gave all humanity to Him, to be used for His own will."[68] She believed that, because of Mary, "God fell in love with humanity."[69] God falling in love with humanity is most concretely seen when Jesus dies on the Cross: "As He looked down from the Cross, with eyes already full of death, Christ saw a huge crowd of people around Him. For these people He was dying."[70]

Houselander also emphasizes the individual. Christ died, not for the crowd, but for each person *in* the crowd. Mary's yes allowed God to take flesh and fall in love with humanity to the point of dying out of love for each soul that would ever live. In that crowd on Calvary, Jesus saw Mary, and spoke to her, telling her to behold John, and in essence Jesus says, "Behold each one of these people as your children." She beholds us now and sees Christ in us and

[68] Houselander, *The Reed of God*, 68.
[69] Houselander, *The Reed of God*, 82.
[70] Houselander, *The Reed of God*, 130.

loves us as her children. Just as God fell in love with humanity because of Mary, because of God, Mary has fallen in love with all of humanity.

One of the reasons why people love Caryll Houselander's *The Reed of God* is because she makes Mary personable. At the very beginning of the book, Caryll says that many people have the wrong idea of Our Lady. She is just the beautiful woman on the Christmas card. She's not human, not *real*. Houselander makes Mary real. She helps us realize that how Mary lived her life is how we should live ours. Ours is a life of imitating Mary. We live our lives like Mary, saying yes to God. We live united to the Holy Spirit. Like her, we surrender to God. Mary "led the Christ life perfectly; her life was literally, as ours should be, 'in Christ.'"[71] As we imitate Mary and live like her, we become her devoted sons and daughters. Houselander summarized it quite well:

> Devotion to Our Lady is the treasure of the Catholic Church. If proof were wanting that she is Christ's church, none could be surer than this. She has never ceased, all through the ages of Christianity, to foster this tender love for the Mother of God. As soon as a child can walk, he walks to Our Lady's altar and puts one more candle to shine among the countless candles at her feet, one more bunch of flowers from the fields is pushed into her hand or laid across gilded shoes; and when he is old and nodding before the altar, it is the same thing. Every trifling this is told to her and every great sorrow; she is the sharer of all earth's joys and griefs.... For each one of us is 'another Christ'; each one, to Mary, is her only child. It is therefore

---

[71] Houselander, *The Reed of God*, 96.

not tedious to her to hear the trifles that we tell her, to look at the bruises that we bring to her, and seeing our wound of sin, to heal it.[72]

When we realize that Mary is real and relatable, it is then that we will truly honor her and love her as our mother. It is then that we will bring to her our joys and sorrows and converse with her like a child.

How to Love Mary Like Caryll Houselander

• Houselander loved the Akathist Hymn to the Theotokos, which she encountered while worshipping in the Russian Orthodox Church. Find the hymn online and pray it. As you read it or listen to it, what are your impressions of this great prayer from the Christian Eastern tradition?
• Houselander's treatment of Advent helps us appreciate the liturgical season of Advent but also the other moments of waiting and silence in our life. Meditate on the advent you find yourself in right now.
• Reflect on the fifth Joyful Mystery and pray about how you have lost Jesus in your life.

[72] Houselander, *The Reed of God*, 163–164.

Lesson 18

Lead with Mary

Pope Francis

People often remember notable events from history. Generations older than me will tell you where they were when Apollo 13 crashed or John F. Kennedy was shot. My generation remembers where they were on September 11, 2001. There are significant events that happen in the Church, and we might also remember where we were when we heard the news. How did you hear the announcement that Pope Benedict was choosing to resign at the end of February 2013? Or where were you when news broke that an Argentinian cardinal named Jorge Bergoglio was elected the supreme pontiff, taking the name Francis? I was on a ten-week parish internship in my diocese. I watched the news break with the pastor of the parish, and we celebrated the fact that *sede vacante* was over. We had a pope.

The pastor and I listened as the new Holy Father addressed the world. One of the requests he made that day was to ask the world to pray that the Virgin Mary would protect him. He then led everyone in the Our Father, Hail Mary, and Glory Be. Afterward, he stated that the following day he would be visiting the Basilica of St. Mary Major and pray before the image of Salus Populi Romani, or Our Lady, Health of the Roman People.

Francis has kept up these visits to the Madonna of Rome throughout his papacy. He visits the image of Our Lady and bows his head in prayer before and after every visit he takes to another country. It is a pious act of devotion, by which he continues to beg Mary's protection and to entrust to her the work he will undertake for the greater glory of God. In a book-length interview titled *Ave Maria: The Mystery of a Most Beloved Prayer*, theologian Marco Pozza asked him about these visits. Pope Francis remarked, "I often came to Rome for a synod or a meeting of the dicasteries of which I was a member. I would go to the churches I knew: Saint Peter's the Gesù, Saint Ignatius, and Saint Mary Major. I often went to Saint Mary Major. I don't know why, but Our Lady, the Mother, has always drawn me. What do I think of when I look at Mary? I go back a bit to the experience with the Virgin of Guadalupe in Mexico: it is certainly wonderful to look at Our Lady, but it is even more wonderful to let Our Lady look at us, to let her look at us and to tell her everything, knowing that she is looking at us."[73] He approaches these meetings as a son visiting his Mother.

Our Lady, Undoer of Knots, is another devotion to Mary that captured the heart of Pope Francis and also allows him to converse with Mary about the struggles he faces. He became familiar with the image of Our Lady, Undoer of Knots, which depicts the Blessed Mother holding a white string with knots, when he visited the Church of St. Peter am Perlach in Augsburg. The story behind the painting dates back to the 1600s when Wolfgang Langenmantel and his wife, Sophie, experienced problems in their marriage. Wolfgang turned to the Jesuit priest Jakob Rem, who prayed to Our Lady while holding the marriage ribbon used to tie the knot of marriage. He

---

[73] Pope Francis, *Ave Maria: The Mystery of a Most Beloved Prayer* (New York: Image Books, 2018), 86.

prayed that the other knots causing the marriage trouble would be untied. The prayer of the priest was heard by God through Mary's intercession, and this image of Mary was commissioned as an act of thanksgiving. A relatively unknown Marian devotion gained prominence when Pope Francis referenced the image. Almost overnight, the Catholic faithful began invoking the intercession of Our Lady, Undoer of Knots. Her image was widely reproduced. Medals were created, novena and prayer pamphlets drafted. Today, it is a devotion to Mary popular with so many who are facing difficulties.

Of course, the idea of Mary as undoing knots is theologically sound. Taught by an early Church Father, St. Irenaeus of Lyons, he contrasted Eve's knot of disobedience to Mary's untying of the knot by her faith and obedience to God's will. As Pope Francis reminds us, "All knots of the heart, all knots of the conscience can be undone. Do I ask Mary that she may help me to trust in God's mercy, to undo them, to change?"[74] The question Pope Francis poses is one worthy for our own reflection.

There are several other devotions to Mary that have influenced Pope Francis. While he was archbishop of Buenos Aires, he would often be a pilgrim and celebrant of Mass at the Shrine of Our Lady of Lujan, the patroness of Argentina. According to legend, in 1630 a rancher was moving the image of Our Lady to his ranch. On the journey, the oxen stopped and would not move until the statue was removed from the wagon. This was taken as a sign that Our Lady wanted to have a shrine built in that spot. During his papacy, Pope Francis has venerated an image of Our Lady of Lujan at the Vatican.

Likewise, Pope Francis's call to missionary discipleship was inspired by another Latin American Marian devotion: Our Lady of Aparecida. This Brazilian shrine to the Blessed Mother was graced

---

[74] Pope Francis, *Ave Maria*, 102.

to have Pope Francis visit during World Youth Day in 2013. While there, Pope Francis remarked that he entrusted his pontificate to her maternal intercession.

Devotion to Our Lady of Aparecida dates back to 1717, when fishermen pulled a statue of Mary out of the water with their nets. Afterward, they pulled in a large catch of fish.

Pope Francis likewise welcomed the statue of Fatima to the Vatican during the centenary of the apparitions and went as a pilgrim to the shrine in Portugal. Similarly, the statue of Our Lady of Knock was flown to the Vatican for a special celebration, and the shrine in Ireland welcomed Pope Francis during his visit for the World Meeting of Families. As pope, Francis has been a devotee of Our Lady, encouraging devotion to her authentic apparitions, which lead us to Jesus.

In June 2020, Pope Francis added a few devotional titles of Mary to the Litany of Loreto. During his pontificate, he called an extraordinary jubilee called the Year of Mercy. As a reminder of that special grace-filled year, the title Mother of Mercy was added. Mother of Hope was another title added to the litany, and also Solace of Migrants. Pope Francis has a special devotion to the poor and caring for them as Christ calls us. For a pope who embraces poverty, it seems only appropriate for him to lead us in devotion to Our Lady as the Solace of Migrants.

In addition to adding titles to the Litany of Loreto, Pope Francis also gave the Church two additional feasts in honor of the Blessed Mother. Fittingly, he added the feast of Mary, Mother of the Church, instructing that it be celebrated the Monday after Pentecost. On the feast of Pentecost, Mary gathered with the Apostles in the Upper Room as the Spirit filled the members of the nascent Church. Mary becomes a mother to all believers. The Church is a mother, too, and learns her motherhood and tenderness from the example of Mary.

The second feast added by Pope Francis was the celebration of Our Lady of Loreto. In 1919, Our Lady of Loreto was named the patroness of pilots and air travel because of the belief that Mary's home was transported to Loreto. As an extension of the jubilee year, to celebrate this designation Pope Francis added the memorial to the universal calendar. It is observed on December 10 each year.

Pope Francis began his pontificate by leading us in prayer to the Virgin Mother of God. He has continued to lead the Church by Mary's prayers and example to a deeper encounter with our Eucharistic and Merciful Lord. He has led us to new devotions to Mary and has prescribed universally new titles and feasts of Our Lady. During the COVID-19 pandemic, he also wrote a prayer to Mary and encouraged the faithful to recite it often. The prayer ends:

We seek refuge under your protection, O Holy Mother of God. Do not despise our pleas—we who are put to the test—and deliver us from every danger, O glorious and blessed Virgin.

How to Love Mary Like Pope Francis

• Imitate Pope Francis in visiting an image of Our Lady, maybe at your parish, before a major trip or project. Talk to Mary about your undertaking.
• Learn more about Our Lady, Undoer of Knots. Pray a novena asking Mary to untie whatever knots you face in your life. You may even ask her to untie the knots of which you are unaware!
• Learn about the shrines of Our Lady of Lujan and Our Lady of Aparecida.

Lesson 19

Challenging Words to Live

Chiara Lubich

My introduction to the Focolare Movement, founded by Chiara Lubich, was through a teenage member of the movement, Chiara Luce Badano, a young girl who was beatified in 2010. I heard of Chiara Luce's story through a priest friend who wanted to attend her beatification in Rome. I was in the seminary, which made it impossible for me to go. I read the young girl's story and was moved by her devotion and love for Jesus. I like telling people I knew Chiara Luce *before* she went viral in the Catholic world.

Chiara Luce was an active young woman who enjoyed playing tennis. One day in 1988, when she was sixteen years old, she felt a pain in her arm. It was not tennis elbow but the beginnings of osteogenic sarcoma, an agonizing form of bone cancer. She immediately embraced the Catholic belief of redemptive suffering. She experienced excruciating pain, but she offered that pain to Jesus for the salvation of souls, especially for young people.

Chiara Luce died two years later at the age of eighteen. When she departed this life, she had a depth of spirituality most of us could only dream of. She loved Jesus with all her heart and loved the person who was before her as Jesus in her midst. Impressed by this young member of the Focolare Movement, I wanted to know who formed her spirituality.

When I was in major seminary, I wanted to write a paper on redemptive suffering. I chose to highlight the life of Blessed Chiara Luce with the thought of Pope St. John Paul II's encyclical on suffering. My research and inquiry would lead me to the foundress of the Focolare Movement, a different Chiara, Chiara Lubich. It was a discovery that would be life changing.

When I began reading Chiara Lubich, it was as if she were speaking to the depths of my soul. She challenged me to be a better Christian and follower of Jesus. I began attending Word of Life meetings each month in Mundelein while I was a seminarian and then in Appleton during my first years of priesthood. Part of the Focolare Spirituality was a monthly focus on living a passage of Sacred Scripture—the Word of Life. At these meetings, we would read the Word of Life, followed by a reflection from Chiara Lubich. Then we'd share what the readings meant to each of us in the room.

I recall one time when I was in Belgium, I stayed at the rectory of a Focolare priest. I shared with him my difficulties in paying for petrol in Europe because it was right at the time when credit cards were transitioning to chips. I couldn't pay at the pump. He sensed I was nervous about filling up before arriving at the airport with my rental car, so he took me to the nearest gas station and paid for my fuel. When I went to pay him, he refused because that month's Word of Life was to give drink to the thirsty. He saw this as an opportunity to live that Word of Life.

Another time, I had hit a breaking point one evening and went to a nearby adoration chapel. I shared with the Lord everything I was experiencing and thinking. I brought with me one of Chiara Lubich's spiritual books. I opened the book and began reading.

The words I read brought me immediate consolation and helped me to move on from the experience.

The Focolare Movement was born in the bomb shelters of World War II. In 1943, a group of women gathered to read Scripture and wanted to begin living the Word in their lives. But the seeds were planted in Lubich's soul years earlier, in 1939. That year, she traveled to Loreto as part of a retreat sponsored by Catholic Action. Being in Loreto afforded Chiara the opportunity to pray in the Holy House. Her prayer was enriched by reflecting on the Annunciation and the life of the Holy Family. She visited the Holy House each day so that she could live with the Holy Family of Nazareth. It was in these moments of prayer that the idea of the Focolare Movement took root in her soul, as she wanted to live a life completely dedicated to God. But she wanted to act as a laywoman, not a nun, anticipating the Second Vatican Council's call for a more active and engaged laity.

Another name for the Focolare Movement is the Work of Mary. The spirituality of the movement focuses much on Jesus Forsaken, who from the Cross cried out to the Father, "Why have you forsaken me?" The Marian counterpart is known as Mary Desolate: Our Lady standing at the foot of the Cross. One of the reasons the Focolare Movement is called the Work of Mary is because Chiara Lubich received in prayer one day the message that they were to be another Mary. She wrote:

I went into church one day, and with my heart full of trust, I asked: "Why did you wish to remain on earth, in the most sweet Eucharist, and you have not found—you who are God—also a way to bring and to leave here Mary, the mother of all of us who journey?" In the silence he seemed to reply, "I have not left her because I want to see her again in you. Even if you are not immaculate, my love

will virginize you, and you, all of you, will open your arms
and hearts as mothers of humanity, which as in times past,
thirsts for God and for his mother. It is you who now must
sooth pains, sooth wounds, dry tears. Sing her litanies and
strive to mirror yourself in them."[75]

According to this prayer experience of Chiara, Jesus wants to
find Mary in us. St. Louis de Montfort says something very similar
about our relationship with the Holy Spirit—that the Spirit makes
His home in the heart of a person who loves Mary.

Chiara's mission is to help each and every one of us become
"Marys" in our own way. We look to Our Lady's virtues and how
she exemplified faith, hope, love, obedience, chastity, and humility.
This is perhaps why Chiara proposes the *Via Mariae*, or the Way
of Mary, focusing on the different episodes of Mary's life and their
relationship to the movement's spirituality: the Annunciation, Visitation, Nativity of Jesus, Presentation, Flight into Egypt, Loss of Jesus
in the Temple, the Intimate Life of Nazareth, the Entry into Public
Life, her Desolation, her time in the Cenacle, and her Assumption
into Heaven. The life or way of Mary is an informative method of
looking to Mary's example and can help form each of us as disciples.

There was one powerful Marian meditation of Chiara Lubich's
that has been a recurring thought, meditation, and reminder in
my own life. When writing about the entrustment of Mary to
John, she wrote:

And from that hour the disciple took her into his home. So
the task of the Church and every Christian is to take Mary
home, live with Mary, and go to Christ with and through

---

[75] Chiara Lubich, *Mary: The Transparency of God* (Hyde Park, NY:
New City Press, 2003), 107.

Mary. She is our spiritual mother, a mother who nourishes
Christians with salvation that is born from her womb, as
Augustine says.... This thought can revolutionize the lives
of many Christians. We love Mary, we pray to her, and we
have pictures of her in our homes. There are churches and
monuments built in her honor. She is present in the Catholic Church and in other churches, and in the hearts of the
faithful. But we do not usually think it is our duty to take
Mary into our homes and live with her as John did. So great
a mother can feed our undernourished Christianity and en-
lighten us with her advice. We could live in the presence of
she who is so much the highest perfection of motherhood.[76]

After encountering these words, I began to live my life daily
with the reminder to take Mary into my home. Such a notion
makes Mary more personal. We will want to talk to our mother
about our day and ask her motherly advice. We will want to please
our mother by our actions. External devotion is not enough. Our
devotion to Mary must become internal and make a difference in
our life by word and action.

Chiara Lubich internalized the Word of God. She meditated
on the Word and shared it with the Focolare Movement. She
and so many have tried to live the Word of Life. The words of
Scripture are challenging. The task Chiara Lubich invites us to is
equally challenging.

Be another Mary. Live with Mary. Love Mary.

[76] Lubich, *Mary: The Transparency of God*, 45.

How to Love Mary Like Chiara Lubich

• Spend some time meditating on the life of Mary. What inspires you most? Perhaps it is her home life in Nazareth. What would it have been like to live with Joseph, Mary, and Jesus?

• Just as the Focolare Movement proposes a word of Scripture to live each month, discover the words of Mary in the Gospels. "Let it be done to me according to your word." "My soul proclaims the greatness of the Lord." "Do whatever he tells you." Be intentional about living one of these phrases for the next few weeks.

Lesson 20

To Think Deeply about Mary

St. Thomas Aquinas

Any person who studies theology will eventually be introduced to St. Thomas Aquinas. His masterpiece, the *Summa Theologica*, was written as an introductory text for students but came to be known as the rule and standard for Christian theology and philosophy.

Ironically, for his great learning, Aquinas came down on the wrong side of one of the most important Marian theological disputes of Church history. Like most Dominicans of the time, Aquinas believed that Mary experienced sanctification in the womb like Jeremiah or St. John the Baptist. He understands Mary being cleansed of Original Sin through sanctification in the womb, but he is unable to arrive at a complete preservation from original sin—what we now know as the Immaculate Conception.

One dogma that Aquinas did champion, however, is the perpetual virginity of Mary. Most Christians understand that Mary was a virgin before the birth of Jesus, as she herself attests to the archangel Gabriel. Yet Mary's virginity after the birth of Jesus can be defended too.

Opponents of the dogma will often cite Jesus being called the firstborn son, that Joseph didn't know Mary until she brought forth

Jesus, and thirdly the naming of brothers and sisters of the Lord in the Gospels. Aquinas quotes Jerome, who says that the word *until* "has a twofold sense in scripture. For sometimes it indicates a fixed time.... On the other hand, it sometimes indicates an indefinite time."[77] When it comes to the brothers and sisters of the Lord, Jerome teaches that the biblical word used for brothers and sisters could mean distant relatives.

I have been asked in many Q&A sessions why it was necessary for Mary to remain a virgin after the birth of Christ. It's not a bad question. Thomas cites a few reasons in the third article of question twenty-eight. He says that Mary's womb becomes a shrine since it housed the incarnate Son of God. Should there be other relations, it would be an act of desecration. Another reason is that if Joseph and Mary had more children, they would appear ungrateful for receiving the Savior of the World into their care. Thirdly, Joseph would presume against the Holy Spirit, because he knew it was by the power of the Holy Spirit that Mary conceived.

The doctrine of *in partu* virginity (or virginity during birth) is the one that causes most people to scratch their heads. What does it mean? The Church states the teaching but does not define it. Often the birth of Christ is analogized to the closed gate, or Christ passing through the doors of the Upper Room. Aquinas affirms three reasons for the fittingness of this belief, saying it was "in keeping with a property of Him whose Birth is in question, for He is the Word of God." According to St. Thomas, "He came for this purpose, that He might take away our corruption. Wherefore it is unfitting that in His Birth He should corrupt His mother's virginity." Finally, "He who commanded us to honor our father and mother should not in His Birth lessen the honor due to His

---

[77] *Summa Theologica*, III, q. 28, art. 3, reply obj. 3.

Mother."[78] The preservation of Mary's virginity before, during, and after the birth of Christ is a long-held Catholic belief that St. Thomas Aquinas helps us defend.

Most people don't think about the Immaculate Conception except on December 8, or Mary's threefold perpetual virginity. Aquinas asking and answering these questions, though, helps us to better understand the person of Mary and deeply think about her as a woman who said yes to God's will for her life. The truths illuminated by St. Thomas in the *Summa* belong not only to theologians, but to the whole Church — for by learning more about Christ's mother, we draw nearer to Christ Himself.

How to Love Mary Like St. Thomas Aquinas

- What deep questions do you have about Mary? Write them down and then try to find the answers through reading, searching, and study.
- The University of Dayton's Marian Library has an "All About Mary" page with many different topics about Mary. Read a few articles and deepen your knowledge.
- The popular writer and podcaster Matt Fradd has authored a nine-day "Marian Consecration with Aquinas." If you want to think about Mary with the mind of Aquinas, this might be the right devotional for you. Aquinas wrote a prayer of entrustment or consecration to Mary which you may wish to pray right now. (See appendix 5.)

---

[78] *Summa Theologica*, III, q. 28, art. 2.

Lesson 21

Mary Was with Her

St. Mariam of Jesus Crucified

One of the highlights of my formation at Mundelein Seminary was the opportunity to spend roughly ten weeks in the Holy Land. During those ten weeks we made our home base in three loca-tions—Bethlehem, Nazareth, and Jerusalem. In Bethlehem, the religious house we stayed at neighbored a Carmelite monastery. This monastery was founded under the inspiration of St. Mariam of Jesus Crucified. During our three weeks in Bethlehem, I visited the chapel of those sisters almost daily, and in their chapel was a large reliquary containing a relic of St. Mariam. I didn't know much about her, but I knew that residing next door to the body of a saint was an opportunity for prayer that I couldn't pass up.

St. Mariam was born in 1846 in Israel, as a result of the Blessed Virgin's intercession. Her parents had suffered the loss of all their children at birth or shortly thereafter. They longed to have a happy, healthy child. Trusting in God, they decided they would visit the Church of the Nativity in Bethlehem. They were certain that Mary would intercede for them—and she did.

Sadly, Mariam's parents died only a few years later, and the orphan was entrusted to the care of her uncle and aunt. Mariam desired to give her life to God as a virgin, but the cultural norms did not allow for this. Her family had arranged a marriage. Mariam persevered in prayer to the Blessed Virgin, asking for guidance in how to avoid this marriage. The night before the wedding, she received the inspiration she needed. She was to cut her hair, which would make her unattractive to her fiancé. Then he would not want to marry her. Her plan succeeded, which infuriated her family. She fled their home and met up with a Muslim family, but her vocal commitment to the Christian faith outraged them and nearly cost Mariam her life: when she left their home, too, she was followed and her throat was slashed, and she was left for dead.

Mariam later recounted that during this time she had a vision of Heaven and saw Mary, the angels, and the saints. Meanwhile, she was being nursed back to life by a mysterious woman who she concluded was the Blessed Virgin Mary. This lady sewed up her wound, which left a scar. Mariam's voice was hoarse throughout her life. Yet the Virgin Mary succeeded in nursing the young girl back to life and told her: "Remember, Mariam, don't act like other people who think they never have enough. Say always, 'That's enough!' Always be content in spite of what you may have to suffer." This was a divine lesson that Mariam learned from the Blessed Virgin herself and one that she never forgot.

During Mariam's recuperation with Our Lady after the encounter, Mary told her that she would become a religious sister—first as a daughter of St. Joseph but later as a daughter of St. Teresa. This in fact came to pass. Once Mariam was able to resume her life, she worked in family homes as a housekeeper, though she was never reunited with her family from whom she'd fled. She entered the first congregation of sisters, but the community discerned it was not God's will for her to make her profession. This led her to the Carmelite monastery of Pau near Lourdes in France. She made her profession and then helped establish a Carmelite monastery in Mangalore.

St. Mariam then received the inspiration to build a Carmelite monastery in Bethlehem. This came to pass, and it was here that St. Mariam ended her days as a religious — in the city of David, where Christ was born, where her parents petitioned Almighty God by the intercession of the Blessed Virgin for a child. It was through her monastic life that Mariam, in her poem "Mary, Mother of the Resurrection," captures Mary's role in the monastery. In it, she repeats over and over: "At the feet of Mary, I found life again."

St. Mariam was privileged with many encounters with the miraculous. She was a stigmatist, and she experienced trances and ecstasies that would keep her in prayer for hours on end. She levitated at times. She experienced a piercing of her heart, which is called transverberation, out of her love for Christ. She had the gift of prophecy, foretelling events that would happen to individuals and countries. And she could read others' hearts, helping people to bring whatever troubled them to God in prayer. She also had an intense love for the Holy Spirit and received inspired words for priests in prayer about devotion to the third Person of the Trinity. She penned a prayer to the Holy Spirit, which fittingly includes Mary, who was spouse of the Holy Spirit.

> Holy Spirit, inspire me.
> Love of God, consume me.
> Along the right path, guide me.
> Mary, my Mother, look down upon me.
> With Jesus, bless me.
> From all harm, all illusion, all danger, preserve me.

St. Mariam also battled the presence of evil in her life. She experienced diabolical attacks and was even possessed by the devil.

God permitted her to experience these things to be more fervent in her prayer. At the end of one these experiences, on September 4, 1868, she prayed, "My Mother: I beg of you the triumph of the Church! Do you know what I am asking of you? The conversion of sinners and the triumph of the Church!" She also saw the virtues of Mary as powerful in conquering evil, most especially Mary's obedience: "The Blessed Mother let it be known to me that obedience always preserves us from every misfortune and from all the snares of Satan."

St. Mariam of Jesus Crucified died from cancer in 1878 after having dedicated her life to loving God with the help of the Blessed Virgin Mary. Her life of mysticism afforded her moments of encounter with Heaven that none of us will experience on this earth. God chose this special soul to share a message with the world and to communicate the divine presence to all people.

Blessed Mariam loved the Virgin Mary. She saw her several times throughout her life, and she lifted her voice asking her prayers. Just as St. Mariam experienced the presence of Mary in her life, we experience a similar presence as our Mother draws near us, sees our needs, and prays for us before our Triune God.

How to Love Mary Like St. Mariam of Jesus Crucified

• Do you know a couple struggling to have a baby? Ask Our Lady to pray for them just as Mariam's parents prayed for her conception and healthy birth.
• Mariam experienced the care of the Blessed Virgin Mary in a physical way as she recovered from her near-death experience. Reflect on how in subtle ways Mary has taken care of you in a spiritual way.

- Pray about Mary's connection to the Holy Spirit, and then pray St. Mariam's prayer to the Holy Spirit.
- How can Mary help you when you face temptations in your life?
- St. Mariam was a poet. Write a poem in honor of Our Lady.

The Rosary Is Meant for Family Prayer

Fr. Patrick Peyton

"The family that prays together, stays together."

"A world at prayer is a world at peace."

You've probably heard both these phrases. However, you probably *didn't* know that they were spoken by Fr. Patrick Peyton, CSC—a man who dedicated his entire life to family prayer, especially through the power of the Rosary. Fr. Peyton belonged to the Order of the Holy Cross, the same religious congregation that runs the University of Notre Dame in Indiana. Fr. Peyton spent time at Notre Dame and recounted a visit to their famous Lourdes Grotto in his memoir *All for Her*.

During a 2019 visit to Massachusetts, I was able to visit the grave of Fr. Peyton. I also had the opportunity to interview Fr. Willy Raymond for my podcast, *How They Love Mary*, about the recently rereleased edition of Fr. Peyton's autobiography. Reading *All for Her* was the shot in the arm I needed. The priestly witness of Fr. Peyton and how he responded to God's will for his life renewed deep within me priestly fervor and zeal for souls. Fr. Peyton's passion for family prayer and the Rosary is contagious, and after encountering this priest who gave everything for Mary, your devotion to the Rosary certainly will be deepened.

Fr. Peyton was born in Ireland to his devout parents in 1909. His father would lead the Rosary each night, instilling within Fr. Peyton the belief that all fathers should lead their families in prayer. Promoting the family Rosary in particular became the passion of Fr. Peyton's life, leading him all around the world for the Family Rosary Apostolate. Just as Billy Graham and others were filling football stadiums for their movements, so, too, was Fr. Peyton known throughout the world. He believed that by praying the Rosary together families could overcome whatever trials they faced. If family life was in trouble, for example, a couple contemplating divorce, he encouraged praying the Rosary together. For Fr. Peyton, there was no problem that the Rosary could not solve.

The witness of family prayer in his home in Ireland influenced this charismatic priest's devotion to promoting the family Rosary. But it was an experience of illness that propelled Fr. Peyton to pledge his entire life to Our Lady. After joining the Holy Cross Fathers, Peyton fell ill with tuberculosis in 1938. His prognosis was not promising. Even if he survived, his doctors said he would never be fully active again.

Fr. Peyton's superior, Fr. Cornelius Hagerty, addressed him about faith in Our Lady's intercession. He said:

> Our Lady will be as good as you think she is. If you think she is a fifty per-center, that is what she will be; if you think she is a hundred per-center, she will be for you a hundred per-center. No one of us ever does as much as he is capable of doing. We always fall short, stopping on the near side of our total effort. Even Our Lord and Our Lady do not do as much as they could do but the reason

is that we think they are not able. We limit them by the extent of our faith.[79]

This spiritual pep talk awakened within Fr. Peyton an awareness of the realness of Mary and her presence and power if only he believed. He entrusted to Mary his total and complete healing and promised that if he was ordained, he would spend his entire life spreading devotion to the Holy Rosary.

As he remained bedridden for some time, he continued his prayers to Mary, prayed in front of images of Our Lady in his room, and blessed himself with Lourdes water. At Peyton's insistence, because he believed he was healed, he asked to be reexamined. The doctors reviewed his test results and determined Peyton could return to a seminormal lifestyle in January 1940. Peyton would be ordained a priest in 1941, a grace that Our Lady obtained for him. Consequently, he devoted his life to spreading the family Rosary, traveling all over the world, something a man who suffered his illness certainly could not accomplish without the grace of God.

In addition to the Family Rosary Crusade, which he led, he also initiated Family Theater Productions, with the aim of bringing together Hollywood actors and actresses to lead the Rosary. Bing Crosby became his most notable ally. Another aim of Family Theater Productions was to produce videos capturing each of the Rosary mysteries. These films influenced many who watched them. One person commented, "I never understood before how Our Lady had suffered for me on Calvary."[80] Another scene described by Peyton in his autobiography struck me and influenced my meditation. For the mystery of Mary's Assumption, Peter, at the bedside of Mary, tells her to tell

---

[79] Fr. Patrick Peyton, *All for Her*, 78.
[80] Peyton, *All for Her*, 256.

Jesus how much he loved Him.[81] Mary, who soon would be reunited with her Son in Heaven, brings a message from earth to her Son, a reminder of Jesus' thrice-asked question, "Do you love me?" All those years later, in the creative genius of this Rosary-mystery film, Peter was still remorseful and renewing his love for the one whom he denied.

The Rosary was Fr. Peyton's whole life. In a sense, he experienced the mysteries of the Rosary personally. He was a tireless promoter of Our Lady, traveling the globe to lead people in praying the Holy Rosary—the devoted son of Our Lady who was healed by her intercession and, in return, devoted his life to her.

On June 3, 1992, as he closed his eyes in death, he uttered the name of Mary. Could it be that she, whom he loved, came to him at the end of his life to bring him to Jesus?

How to Love Mary Like Fr. Patrick Peyton

- Pray the Rosary with at least one other person. If you're married or live with your parents, pray it together. If you are a religious community, pray it together. If you are a college student, find another student to pray it with. Often, we pray the Rosary alone, but Fr. Peyton would want us to pray the Rosary together.
- One of Fr. Peyton's favorite Marian prayers was the Memorare. He prayed it often and had recourse to it when he needed direction. Pray the Memorare today.
- There is a beautiful film on the life of Fr. Peyton called *Pray*. Make it a family movie night and afterward pray the Rosary together.

[81] Peyton, *All for Her*, 243.

Lesson 23

The Use of Imaginative Prayer When Receiving Holy Communion

Fr. Daniel Lord, SJ

Fr. Daniel Lord isn't a household name, not even with Catholics—at least, not anymore. In the first half of the 1900s, he was one of the most popular priests in America. He was a prolific author. It is said he wrote over a million words in his life. He published in all different genres: long treatises, short pamphlets, devotional works, even children's books. His apostolate involved the Queen's Work from St. Louis. He was also a popular priest in show business and authored the Hollywood Code of Ethics.

I discovered Fr. Lord by accident. I was perusing the stacks of a theological library, searching for a topic that I could write a paper on and present at an academic conference. The focus of the conference was Mary and the Sacraments of Initiation. I thought that maybe I would write about the Prayers after Communion found in hand missals of yesteryear. As I was looking through books, one caught my eye. The title on the spine said, *Christ in Me*. The book contained guided meditations by Fr. Lord. About a fifth of them pertained to the Blessed Mother. I decided I needed to learn about Fr. Lord.

Of Fr. Lord's vast writings about the Catholic Faith, two specifi-
cally pertain to the Virgin Mary: *The Song of the Rosary* and *Mary in
the Modern World*. *Christ in Me* has several reflections about receiving Holy Communion in union with Mary, in imitation of Mary,
and calling to mind her last Holy Communion. He also penned a
few novena booklets in honor of Our Lady and her apparitions. I
immersed myself in his writings, and here are a few ways that Fr.
Lord taught me to love Mary in new ways.

Fr. Lord influenced my Marian meditation by employing imagi-
native prayer and brought about a new way I could love Mary. St.
Ignatius of Loyola, founder of the Jesuits, taught this style of prayer,
by which a person places themselves in the stories told in Scripture.

As I made my way through Fr. Lord's writings, two things made
a huge impression on me. *The Song of the Rosary*, written in a style
of lyrical poetry, offers fresh reflections on the mysteries of the
Rosary. While reflecting on the first Sorrowful Mystery, Christ's
agony in the garden, we get a glimpse of the Last Supper, before
Jesus goes off to the Garden only to be betrayed by a kiss and ar-
rested. Fr. Lord wrote:

> Lanthorn aloft, the Mother crossed the room,
> Lingered a little where He last had sat,
> Shepherd to flock of twelve
> Already stirred by breath upon the wind
> Of nearing wolves.
> A chalice stood where He had laid it down,
> Taken from John,
> The very first to drink,
> The last to hold it for a second to his heart.
> One drop of wine that was no longer wine
> Deep in its crystal throat

She carried to her lips,
Drinking it down
Who once had given blood to fill the veins
Of God within her.
Then reverently she wrapped it in her veil,
Hiding it in a cabinet that stood
Waiting to be the first
Repository.[82]

Another consideration of Lord's Marian Eucharistic imagination is Mary's reception of Holy Communion from the hand of John. This does not seem implausible, given what the Scriptures tell us about the nascent Church in the Acts of the Apostles. In Acts 2:42, we learn that the early Christians devoted themselves to the breaking of the bread. Given that Jesus mandated the apostles to celebrate the Eucharist in remembrance of Him, and the breaking of the bread with Jesus Himself on the road to Emmaus, we can be certain the apostles celebrated the Eucharist together. Since John took Mary into his home, it is no stretch that Mary received the Eucharist from his hand.

This nonbiblical scene of Mary receiving Holy Communion from John has been captured in several artistic renderings, some as paintings and others as stained-glass windows. Of note is the stained-glass triptych in the Dahlgren Chapel of Georgetown University. The three stained-glass windows depict a Johannine theology: John resting on the breast of Jesus at the Last Supper, John's presence at Calvary and the entrustment of Mary to his care, and John administering Holy Communion to Mary. The triptych places

---

[82] Daniel A. Lord, *The Song of the Rosary* (St. Louis, MO: Eucharistic Crusade of the Knights and Handmaids of the Blessed Sacrament), 148.

Christ's sacrifice on Calvary at the center, flanked on both sides by the outpouring of Christ's love through the Holy Eucharist. With Calvary as the focal point, the two sides of the triptych could be seen through this lens. The Last Supper gives way to the Crucifixion and the ultimate offering of Christ's body and blood, while Mary's reception of Holy Communion is Calvary presented again. John giving Mary Holy Communion shows continuity from the Last Supper to Calvary, and Mary's reception of Holy Communion from John hearkens back to their presence at the foot of the Cross.

Fr. Lord makes use of his imagination a third time in his meditation entitled "Thanksgiving in Union with Our Lady's Last Communion." In this meditation, Fr. Lord reflects on Mary's final Communion, that is to say, her Viaticum. Looking to Mary in this regard allows us to anticipate our Christian journey, experience it through and with her, and then ask her to pray for us that we may receive the grace of final Viaticum and all other graces attached to it, including "confidence, love, and complete trust [in] the coming of my Lord."

Fr. Lord also encouraged his readers or hearers to receive Communion with Our Lady, in union with Our Lady, and in imitation of Our Lady. In a few meditations he asks Our Lady, to "give me the truth that makes me know myself, my dependence upon God, the weakness of my soul, and the great condescension of the Savior."[83] In other petitions he asked Our Lady to give him something in particular:

Mary, virgin unsullied, give me the strength to bring to Jesus the purity He loved, the purity that is like you.[84]

---

[83] Fr. Daniel A. Lord, SJ, *Christ in Me* (Milwaukee, WI: Bruce Publishing Company, 1952), 99.

[84] Lord, *Christ in Me*, 100.

Mary, poorest and purest of maids, give me your love of heavenly things, your detachment from earth.[85]

Mary, give me something of the intense love and devotion which was yours when St. John said Mass for you.[86]

Fr. Lord taught me that when I receive Holy Communion, I can petition Mary for her prayers and in so doing, I can better receive the Lord by the help of her prayers and God's grace.

How to Love Mary Like Fr. Daniel Lord

- The next time you go to Mass, after receiving Holy Communion, think about Mary and her reception of Holy Communion. How did she receive Communion? What does it mean for you and your reception of Holy Communion? What petitions could you address to Mary after Holy Communion, deepening your love and appreciation for the sacrament?
- Acquire one of Fr. Lord's pamphlets and pray a novena with him.

---

[85] Lord, *Christ in Me*, 100.
[86] Lord, *Christ in Me*, 105.

Lesson 24

A Simple Approach to Marian Devotion

Blessed Solanus Casey

Bl. Solanus Casey has a certain claim to my diocese of Green Bay, Wisconsin. Though he grew up in the neighboring diocese of La Crosse and spent most of his ministry in Michigan, he celebrated his Mass of Thanksgiving following ordination at St. Joseph Parish in Appleton. Why? Because Solanus was a Capuchin, and Appleton happened to be home to the nearest Capuchin friary!

I heard stories of Fr. Solanus's departure from St. Francis Seminary in Milwaukee due to academic difficulties. My earliest memory of him, though, was quite different. When I was younger, our cat had kittens, and we were hoping to find good homes for them. My childhood pastor adopted one and named the feline Casey, after Solanus Casey.

During my six years in the seminary, I had the opportunity to meet and befriend many of the men from my diocese who also felt called to the priesthood. One in particular had a strong devotion to Venerable Solanus Casey on account of the many miracles people experienced by his intercession, even while he was alive. The young man desired a miracle and began to ask Solanus's prayers. Several years later, he received his miracle. Solanus did it again.

Then came my assignment to a small parish in southern Door County. One of the previous pastors of the parish, who also was a Capuchin, lived with Fr. Solanus Casey for five years. When I read Michael Crosby's book *Thank God Ahead of Time*, I was surprised to come across the name of the parish's former pastor. While at the parish, he inculcated a love for Solanus Casey among some of the parishioners. One of them entrusted a relic badge of Solanus Casey to me on the day I had two teeth extracted in anticipation of getting orthodontics. She told me that Solanus did not like going to the dentist.

While I was aware of small factoids about Solanus—like his popular phrase "thank God ahead of time," which once made for a good Thanksgiving Day homily—I never studied anything else about him. Then it was announced that Solanus would be beatified on November 18, 2017, at Ford Field in Detroit, Michigan. I figured there was no better time to learn about the saintly porter of St. Bonaventure Friary. I acquired his biography and read it on a train ride. I quickly realized that he was a kind of American Padre Pio! And, like St. Pio, he had a deep devotion to the Blessed Virgin Mary.

When he was a boy, Solanus's mother gave him a brown scapular. Reflecting on an episode from his early life, Solanus believed the scapular saved his life. After work one day, a man fell into a pit of water and was drowning. Solanus jumped in, attempting to save the man's life. While being pulled down under the water, he clung to his scapular and was somehow pulled up. Solanus survived this near drowning, but the other man was not as fortunate.

It's interesting that Solanus says he was somehow pulled up, even though he was being plunged under. Was it the hand of Mary, in whose garment he was clothed, that resisted the force of being pulled? Such a conclusion might not be far-fetched. There are many stories available to us pertaining to the scapular's power. Homes have been saved from fire. A scapular dropped in a body of water calmed waters that had seemed dangerous enough to bring about an almost certain death. A bullet became lodged in the scapular, thus preventing death. Given miraculous phenomena in the life of believers, it's possible that Solanus is right: the scapular did indeed save his life. So often we are unaware of the supernatural goings-on all around us.

Another aspect of Solanus Casey's Marian devotion might be connected to the brown scapular. Being enrolled in the Confraternity of the Brown Scapular necessitates living a certain way of life with some expectations. This includes the recitation of the Little Office of the Blessed Virgin Mary, a stipulation that a priest can dispense and require a Rosary instead. The Little Office of the Blessed Virgin Mary has a form similar to the Liturgy of the Hours, which is prayed by clergy, religious, and the faithful. A priest promises daily recitation of the Liturgy of the Hours (also called the breviary or Divine Office). For priests, the Little Office is prayed out of love and devotion, since it would not suffice for their obligation to pray the breviary.

There is a popular image of Fr. Solanus standing near a grotto of Mary, with book in hand, praying. According to a caption I came across, it says Solanus is praying the Little Office. He took this devotion quite seriously, believing that to neglect it would be a sign of his ingratitude toward the Blessed Virgin, who had been so good to him throughout his life.

Solanus felt a call to the priesthood stirring within his soul. After consulting his parish priest, he set out for St. Francis de Sales Seminary in Milwaukee, Wisconsin, to begin his studies. He was a poor student, and the seminary's administration needed to make a decision: should Solanus continue on toward priesthood?

They recommended that he enter a religious order. This brought his priestly discernment to a new level.

Seeking guidance, Solanus prayed a novena in anticipation of the Feast of the Immaculate Conception. As he prayed each day, he discerned that he felt called to live a life consecrated to God. At the very least, he would make a private vow of chastity. Solanus reached a conclusion by the end of the novena, as he felt the maternal presence of Mary and heard the words, "Go to Detroit." The Immaculata interceded for him, and he set off for Detroit to join the Capuchins.

Throughout his life, Fr. Solanus prayed the Rosary often and for special intentions, offering it for those he knew needed his prayers. A friend of Solanus's, Art Lohrman, once shared an anecdote about wanting to spend extra time with Solanus while out for a walk. Art pretended he could not find the bridge to get back home. Solanus recommended praying a Rosary that he might find it and, once they found the bridge, Solanus insisted on praying another Rosary in thanksgiving.

Solanus was also a devoted follower of Venerable Mary of Agreda (1602–1665), a Spanish Conceptionist Poor Clare nun, who was commanded by God to write the life of the Blessed Virgin Mary. Her mystical revelations are contained in the four-volume *The Mystical City of God*. Initially skeptical of Mary of Agreda's claims, Solanus eventually read the entire work three times over the span of forty years, always on his knees. At nearly three thousand pages, it was an accomplishment for any man—let alone one who found reading very difficult, as did Solanus. When death neared, he requested the help of visitors and nurses to read the book to him. If a word or phrase was misread, he knew it and corrected them.

As the hour of death drew near, Solanus sang out a hymn to the Blessed Virgin. His devotion to Mary, which had been kindled in his youth, now burned brighter than ever. His admiration for the Mother of God should inspire us. In fact, Solanus felt strongly about our need for a Marian devotion. He believed that devotion to Mary could help curb the growing atheism and communism of his time. He also encouraged people to "learn to know Mary, that you may love Heaven and heavenly things."

How to Love Mary Like Blessed Solanus Casey

* Acquire a copy of the Little Office. Pray it every day, or on Saturdays (Our Lady's day) and on Marian feast days.
* Pray a novena for nine days leading up to a Marian feast like the Assumption, Immaculate Conception, or the date of a favorite apparition. You might wish to pray a novena before every Marian feast as a way of drawing nearer to Our Lady. Whenever you pray a novena, be sure to have a special intention for which you want to pray.
* The next time you are in the car, whether by yourself or with friends, pray the Rosary.

Lesson 25

What Mary's Feasts Mean for Us

St. Francis de Sales

As a writer myself, I've often relied on the intercession of St. Francis de Sales, the patron saint of writers. Yet I wasn't actually very familiar with his writings. I knew that St. Francis de Sales wrote some spiritual classics, like *Introduction to the Devout Life*, but anything further was unknown to me. This changed one Lenten season. At some point in my book collecting, I added a volume of St. Francis's Lenten sermons to my shelf. Each Lent as a priest I have adopted the practice of reading Lenten homilies by saints to inspire me in my spiritual life and my preaching. His homilies spoke to me, and I incorporated his wisdom into my own sermons.

A year or two later, I interviewed Fr. Thomas Dailey for my podcast *How They Love Mary*, and at the end of the interview, I asked him, "Is there a Marian book you would recommend?"[87] He immediately recommended *On Our Lady: The Sermons of St. Francis de Sales*, which I discovered was still in print. I quickly bought a copy, confident that St. Francis de Sales could inspire my love for

[87] Episode 91, released on June 1, 2021.

Our Lady. My biggest takeaway from reading and meditating on them was the meaning of the liturgical feasts for our life.

Upon opening *The Sermons of St. Francis de Sales: On Our Lady*, the reader encounters first the dedication: "Dedicated to Notre Dame de Bonne Deliverance, Our Lady of Kind Deliverance, at whose feet and through whose intercession St. Francis de Sales was delivered from interior darkness so great that it had brought him to the gates of death."[88] After the preface and preceding the first sermon, an image of Notre Dame de Bonne Deliverance is included, noting that she is "the Black Virgin, through whose intercession St. Francis de Sales was delivered from terrible agony of soul at age nineteen." St. Francis de Sales had a devotion to a particular title and shrine of Our Lady, and being curious, I wanted to know more and learn the story about his healing and the history of this devotion to Our Lady.

The parish church of Saint-Étienne-des-Grès contained a statue of a black Madonna. St. Francis de Sales in his youth, from the age of sixteen to twenty-one, would often pray before this statue of Our Lady. He was struggling with depression, couldn't sleep, was losing weight. He was troubled by the theology of predestination, which was torturing his mind. He feared eternal damnation. As he made daily visits to Our Lady, on one occasion he prayed the Memorare before the statue, and all his mental anguish was lifted from him. Our Lady had broken the chains that held him. Given this grace of freedom, St. Francis de Sales pursued the Lord and Holy Orders, becoming a bishop, a Doctor of the Church, and one of the greatest preachers in France—all thanks to Mary's intercession and deliverance.

---

[88] St. Francis de Sales, *The Sermons of St. Francis de Sales: On Our Lady* (Charlotte, NC: TAN Books, 2013).

The volume of St. Francis de Sales's sermons on Our Lady contains thirteen of the sermons he preached. They were originally delivered to the Daughters of the Visitation, a religious community he founded. His preaching at times is very much tailored to the religious and their state of life. Nevertheless, he offers much for our reflection too.

The feasts of Our Lady teach us different virtues we should cultivate. For example, the feast of Mary's Nativity teaches us re-nunciation because Mary, in her birth, renounced the world, her flesh, and herself.[89] She renounced the world because she was born with a mission to be set apart for God alone. She renounced her flesh because her conception was immaculate and she was not disposed to sin. She renounced herself as she began her life as the Lord's handmaid.

Other virtues held up by St. Francis de Sales were Mary's humil-ity and charity (as evidenced by the Visitation), as well as purity, vir-ginity, and chastity (which are emphasized at the Annunciation).[90] Mary exemplifies obedience to God's will, demonstrated by the Purification of Mary. With all these virtues that Mary provides an example of, St. Francis de Sales encouraged the sisters that "we must take care to imitate her as closely as possible."[91]

In the person of Mary, we realize the areas in which we need growth. Mary as our mother wants to help us. As she looks over all believers, St. Francis de Sales reminds us, "She is the protectress of all people and each vocation in general."[92] Whatever area of your life you are struggling with, entrust it to Mary and know she

[89] St. Francis de Sales, *On Our Lady*, 102.
[90] St. Francis de Sales, *On Our Lady*, 143.
[91] St. Francis de Sales, *On Our Lady*, 82.
[92] St. Francis de Sales, *On Our Lady*, 150.

wants to protect you and help you live out your vocation joyfully and virtuously.

Finally, the feasts of Our Lady remind us that the external is not enough. Our celebration of certain feasts is not sufficient. They must do something for us internally. He writes, "The worldly minded imagine that devotion to Our Lady usually consists in carrying a rosary in their cincture. It seems to them that it is enough to pray it a number of times without doing anything else. In this they are greatly mistaken. For our dear mistress wants us to do what her Son commands us and considers as done to herself the honor we give to her Son by keeping His commandments."[93] Meditating on the life of Jesus and Mary through the Rosary and asking for Mary's prayers now and at the hour of our death has to change our hearts and conform us to Jesus and Mary. If we pray the Rosary and yet live contrarily to the gospel, then our devotion has done nothing for us. De Sales reminds us that when we celebrate Our Lady, we must remember how she lived, imitate her example, and remember her words to us: "Do whatever he tells you." When we take seriously the feasts of Our Lady and celebrate them not only externally but in our heart, and allow them to transform us, then we will be truly celebrating and honoring Our Lady.

How to Love Mary Like St. Francis de Sales

* Make a daily visit to a statue of Our Lady and pray the Memorare. Is there an outdoor statue nearby your home or do you have one in your yard or house?

---

[93] St. Francis de Sales, *On Our Lady*, 195–196.

- Ask Mary to deliver you from any thoughts that are inhibiting you from doing God's will.
- What virtue of Mary do you wish to imitate and implement more in your life?
- In a sermon for the Feast of the Annunciation, St. Francis de Sales sets out to tell us four things about that blessed event: "The first is what we should believe, the second what we should hope for, the third what we should love, and the fourth what we should do and practice." On the next Marian feast, ask these questions of yourself: What is this feast about? How does it give me hope? What am I to love? What am I to do in response?

Give Your Life to Mary

Venerable Aloysius Schwartz

Sometimes in your life you will encounter a saint or holy person by accident. Maybe you will discover a social media post someone shared or happen upon an article. It could be in a book or a podcast. I discovered Venerable Aloysius Schwartz through a radio interview that Kevin Wells did with Gus Lloyd of SiriusXM's The Catholic Channel. I was commuting back from daily Mass to my home office. I got in the car and began to listen to an interview about an American priest who served as a missionary in South Korea. I heard only a few minutes before a commercial break, but I definitely wanted to hear the rest of the story. Why? Because Kevin Wells, author of *Priest and Beggar: The Heroic Life of Venerable Aloysius Schwartz*, had shared about the immense love "Father Al" had for the Virgin Mary.

Born in 1930, Fr. Aloysius had a great love for the poor from an early age. The witness of consecrated life by a relative was influential in his own discernment. Having his eyes and heart set on being a missionary, the young Aloysius joined the Maryknoll order, known for their missionary work throughout the world, especially among the poor. Something didn't feel right to Aloysius about the Maryknoll order, though. What he observed left him unsettled because he believed the order lived too comfortably. They did not embrace the lifestyle of the poor themselves. He believed that if you were to serve the poor, you had to be like them—just as Jesus, the son of God, became poor and lived His life among us.

Aloysius then discovered a foreign missionary order, headquartered in Belgium. He joined the Société des Auxiliaires des Missions (SAM) and pursued Holy Orders with their community. A rift between him and a superior nearly left him in the lay state, but the Virgin Mary spared his vocation, and as a result he entrusted his entire life and ministry to her maternal intercession.

During his time in Belgium, Aloysius became familiar with the Marian apparitions received by Mariette Beco in 1933. He visited the shrine and the grounds several times during his study. It is not surprising he was drawn to this apparition of Our Lady because Mary told Mariette that she was the Virgin of the Poor who came to relieve suffering. Given that he wanted to live as a poor missionary among the poor, it is fitting and appropriate he would take the Virgin of the Poor as his intercessor and patroness. When his ordination hung in the balance, he prayed at the shrine in Banneux, asking Our Lady to help him be ordained. He spoke with a bishop in Belgium, Bishop Kerkhofs, and shared with him his love for the Virgin of the Poor. His devotion impressed the bishop so much that he agreed to support his ordination to the priesthood. He was incardinated into that Belgian diocese, giving Al a new superior and allowing him to part company from the SAM order.

The message Mary gave to Mariette became the mission of Father Al. In the establishment of "Boystowns" and "Girlstowns," he wanted to relieve the suffering and burdens of the poor. Poor children would make their home in these "towns" for a few years, receiving formation in the Christian life and preparation to make a valuable contribution to society.

The Virgin of the Poor was a constant reminder for him and the order of sisters he founded, fittingly called the Sisters of Mary. Behind their motherhouse stood a large statue of Our Lady of Banneux, who kept watch over the community. Throughout his life and ministry, Father Al felt the presence of Our Lady of Banneux and believed she orchestrated all the missionary work he and the sisters undertook. Once, he admitted: "Can I handle all this? No, not really. But I entrust all these plans and projects to the Virgin of the Poor for the glory of God. She will handle it quite well."[94]

Fr. Al truly believed his work was Our Lady's work and he was her servant. He gave everything to Our Lady. This is most evident in a prayer he wrote to the Virgin of the Poor. It begins: "For a long time now I have entrusted to you all that I have and all that I am. You have taken all, I have nothing. *Je suis pauvre.*" He goes on, "I renew — so deeply conscious of what I am, my weakness, my imperfection — the words of consecration: all I have and am — Virgin of the Poor, yes, yes! But O Mother, have pity, I am a beggar and alone, and I am so weary. But I will risk all, all, all."

Of course, Father Al was also devoted to the Holy Rosary. Having embraced a life of poverty, it is said one of his few possessions was his rosary, which he kept in his pocket at all times. His neighbors and those who lived in his village saw him walking around the neighborhood praying the Rosary. When offering counsel to couples before marriage, he would instruct them that the secret to a heathy and long marriage was the daily recitation of the Rosary. He would lead the recitation of the Rosary for the

---

[94] Kevin Wells, *Priest and Beggar: The Heroic Life of Venerable Aloysius Schwartz* (San Francisco: Ignatius Press, 2021), 173.

sisters and for the children at Boystown and Girlstown. In these houses of formation for the poor children, the Rosary would be recited each day at 7:00 p.m., a custom associated with the shrine at Banneux. Since the time of the apparitions, the Rosary has been recited at the shrine in an unbroken succession at 7:00 p.m. daily.

Our Lady of Banneux saved Father Al's vocation and was his constant intercessor since he gave the entirety of his work to her. Near the end of his life, as he continued to expand the mission to new countries, he began to discern the possibility of serving the poor in Mexico. Just as his missionary work began at the feet of Our Lady of Banneux, he now allowed another image of the Madonna to capture his heart: Our Lady of Guadalupe.

After arriving in Mexico, he visited the Shrine of Our Lady of Guadalupe near Mexico City. He felt great uncertainty about the project, and so he laid those fears at her feet, begging for direction. Just as he made a promise to Our Lady in Banneux, he made a similar promise in Guadalupe. He told her he would keep working for her until the day he died. On the feast of Our Lady of the Rosary in 1991, eight hundred children were welcomed into Fr. Al's mission field. His promise to Our Lady was fulfilled. Having been diagnosed with ALS, Fr. Al would soon succumb to the illness, and Our Lady would fulfill her promises to him, as she prayed for him at the hour of his death.

As I read the life of Venerable Aloysius Schwartz, though, one thing continued to strike me: he usually chose to begin a new work or project on a feast of Our Lady. Whether intentional or not, it happened repeatedly, except for his birth and death. He began his missionary work in Seoul on the feast of the Immaculate Conception, December 8, 1957. The second Boystown opened in Korea on January 1, 1975, the solemnity of Mary, Mother of God. The feast of the Assumption, August 15, 1985, saw the beginning of his center for care in Manila. And his missionary work in Mexico started on the feast of Our Lady of the Rosary, October 7, 1991. In the spirit of giving everything to Mary, these important dates served as an act of entrustment to Mary and in honor of the mission he received for his life by her intercession.

How to Love Mary Like Venerable Aloysius Schwartz

- Learn more about Our Lady of Banneux and ask her intercession. A litany to Our Lady of Banneux can be found in Appendix Four.
- Do you have a major life decision approaching? Beginning something new? Bringing an end to something? Look at the church's liturgical calendar and see if there is a feast of Our Lady that you could commemorate in conjunction with your decision.

Lesson 27

Be Joyful with Mary

Sr. Clare Crockett

There's a documentary on Sr. Clare Crockett on YouTube called *All or Nothing* that currently has over 1.8 million views. Though she died only recently, in 2016, devotion to this holy woman is spreading like wildfire.

Indeed, her life and spirituality are quite impressive. Her holiness was contagious. Her joy was apparent. In my opinion, she is the next Bl. Chiara Luce Badano or Bl. Carlo Acutis. As people learn her story, they find an attraction to her life that encourages them to love Jesus more.

Sr. Clare was born on November 14, 1982, in Derry. As a girl, she dreamed of growing up to be a famous actress. Later she admitted that, as a teenager, she dabbled in certain sinful behaviors to which the young are especially inclined. She would be deeply moved to conversion on Good Friday in 2000 and began striving for holiness. This conversion experience was motivated by a pilgrimage and retreat in Spain sponsored by the religious community Home of the Mother. Home of the Mother was founded in the 1980s by Fr. Rafael Alonso Reymundo. Today, they serve throughout the world. Sr. Clare Crockett spent a few years in their Jacksonville,

Florida, apostolate. During that pilgrimage and retreat, the seeds of Clare Crockett's religious vocation already began to blossom. She would join the Servant Sisters of the Home of the Mother, a community with a Eucharistic and Marian spirituality. She made her first vows in 2006. Over the course of her religious life, Sr. Clare allowed the Lord to transform her heart. Those that knew her best were struck by the change. In a few short years, she grew into a living saint.

Her life in religion was cut short by an earthquake in Ecuador. In her teachings, she always emphasized living in a state of grace and being prepared for death. Sr. Clare believed she might die young, at age thirty-three—traditionally, the same age Our Lord was when He died on the Cross.

When a religious sister enters religious life, she might be given a new name or an attribution after her own name, such as "St. Thérèse of the Child Jesus and of the Holy Face." Sr. Clare's full name was "Sr. Clare Maria of the Trinity and of the Heart of Mary." It was during the second year of novitiate that Sr. Clare began fostering a deeper love for the Blessed Mother. There were moments where a glance at a statue of Mary or talking about Mary would fill her with joy. As she prayed about her name, she felt strongly in prayer it was to be "of the Trinity and of the Heart of Mary." She asked God to confirm her feelings with a specific request. She wanted the community to sing the song "Mother, More Beautiful than the Sun." If she was to have a Marian title in her name, they would sing.

Sure enough, they sang. It seems appropriate to quote the English translation of the refrain, which goes:

I want to be yours, Mother,
Yours, always, always.

> May nothing in this world
> Separate me from You.

Sr. Clare made this prayer the refrain of her life.

Marian song was important to Sr. Clare. She wielded a guitar and would lead young people in singing the praises of God and the Blessed Virgin Mary. We all sing songs and have lines memorized. When we attend Mass on Marian feast days, we can probably sing many of the songs from memory. It's important to take time to think about the words that we sing and what they mean. They can be a method of teaching for us, and they can also be an expression of our heart in prayer. Here are the words of a song Sr. Clare wrote to honor Our Lady:

> We all mess up every once in a while
> And we say "no" instead of saying "yes."
> And we end up doing what we shouldn't do.
> In our lives we have seen Her act
> And this is why we want to sing Her this song.
> She comes to rescue us.
> Our Rescuer, faithful Mother.
> Our Rescuer, thank you for your daily help.
> Our Rescuer, do not hide yourself from me, Rescuer.[95]

Sr. Clare was a pilgrim as well as a songwriter. In her home country of Ireland, she was a pilgrim to the apparition site of Knock in County Mayo. She visited Lourdes five or six times. On previous trips she had never entered the baths to allow the miraculous healing water to wash over her body. In March 2012

---

[95] Sr. Kristen Gardner, *Sr. Clare Crockett: Alone with Christ Alone* (New Hope, KY: New Hope Publications, 2021), 268.

that changed, and she resolved to enter the baths for three reasons: "(1) Out of love for Our Lady. (2) To show Her my trust in Her. (3) To be healed from whatever She wants to heal me from."[96] On another pilgrimage, she found herself in the Holy Land and was deeply moved to renew her yes to the Lord in the home of Mary at Nazareth.

Sr. Clare had a passion for teaching young people. In *All or Nothing*, some young people recall the lessons Sr. Clare taught them. She told them that at Adoration for three minutes they should simply look at the monstrance and look at Jesus and allow Jesus to look at them. She believed something powerful could happen in those three minutes. Sr. Clare's love for Mary inspired some schoolchildren to ask her to help them do something more to show their love for Mary. Sr. Clare then began a Rosary Club, teaching this devotion to the children and encouraging them to pray it with their families. While strongly devoted to Mary, in one of Sr. Clare's writings she expressed her sorrow in not loving Mary more by faithfully praying the Rosary: "It hurts me to know that there have been days when I did not show the Virgin my love in this way."[97]

Sr. Clare's presence on YouTube and social media have made her famous in her death. That would have pleased her: when she first decided she was called to be a nun, she would tell people she wanted to be a famous nun. Her life, though shortened by natural disaster, has allowed many people to fall in love with the Lord through her story. One Instagram post on the Brazilian Irma Clare page, translated by Google, communicated Sr. Clare's love for Mary:

[96] Gardner, *Sr. Clare Crockett*, 274.
[97] Gardner, *Sr. Clare Crockett*, 282.

How big the Virgin Mary is! I don't even know how to explain the good it does me to be with Her and just look at Her. She pampers me in a way that leaves me speechless and makes me feel very, very small, because I see that She is the one who guides my life. I asked her for the grace of being crazy about her and being able to do what she always asks me to do.

How to Love Mary Like Sr. Clare Crockett

• Listen to your favorite Marian song or discover a new song about Mary. Listen to the words, learn them, and sing them.
• How has Mary been a rescuer in your life? How has she pampered you, or guided you?
• Ask Mary for the grace of being crazy about her!

Lesson 28

The Little Way of Confidence in Mary

Sr. Teresa of Jesus Quevedo

I hadn't heard of Sr. Teresa, or Teresita, Quevedo until a few weeks before I started writing this book. I was having lunch with the "Saint Ninja," Meg Hunter-Kilmer, and asked for her advice as I filled in the last individuals this book would feature. One thing that has amazed me about Meg is her passion for the obscure and unknown saints in our Church. She beautifully tells their stories in the articles and books she writes and in her Instagram posts. I told her that I felt I needed a few more women as the book featured a lot of priests and bishops throughout Church history. She immediately said I should read about Teresita Quevedo, a Spanish nun who died at a young age.

Sr. Teresita's biography is appropriately titled *Mary Was Her Life*. It was a treat to read, and she's a perfect person to end these profiles of Marian devotion. Page after page was filled with wisdom about Mary. This profile can only capture a snapshot of her love for the Blessed Mother.

Teresita Quevedo was born on April 14, 1930, in Madrid, Spain to Dr. Calixto and Dona Maria Quevedo. The experience of her First Communion was life changing for her. It instilled in her a desire to live a more virtuous life, even as a little girl.

How They Love Mary

Teresita was an excellent swimmer and diver. Coaches sought after her to join their team because they believed she would be a medalist. She declined, as she wanted not to be prideful and to dedicate more time to spiritual practices.

She was educated by the Carmelite Sisters of Charity and a few of her aunts were sisters in the community. During her senior year of high school, Teresita realized a longing within herself to become a nun. She waited until after the Epiphany to tell her family of her intention to enter the religious life the next month. They approved of her decision and let her follow God's will for her life. Likewise, her confessor and the Mother Superior of the congregation strongly supported her vocation.

From a very young age, Teresita had a devotion to Mary. Her father taught her to pray. One of their favorite prayers went "O sweet Virgin Mary, my Mother, I offer myself today completely to you. I beg you to give my body, eyes, ears, and tongue, my heart and soul to Jesus. I am all yours, holy Mother of God. Watch over me! Amen."[98] Throughout her life, when people asked her how she fostered a love for Mary, she would recount this experience with her father and this prayer as the foundation.[99] This short prayer, in which she offered everything to Jesus through the Blessed Virgin Mary, became the bedrock of her devotion to Mary.

The Quevedo home was a house of prayer, and Calixto was the leader of prayer. Each evening, the family would gather around a wood carving of Murillo's *Immaculate Conception* and pray the

---

[98] Sister Mary Pierre Tirrell, RSM, *Mary Was Her Life: The Story of a Nun, Sister Maria Teresa Quevedo, 1930–1950* (Barakaldo Books, 2020), 15.

[99] Tirrell, *Mary Was Her Life*, 184.

Rosary.[100] While in school, she prayed the Sorrowful Mysteries of the Rosary before the Blessed Sacrament, a practice that inspired her classmates.

At her First Communion, Teresita took Mary to be her special companion and patroness. She confided everything of her life to the Blessed Virgin and from her sought heavenly counsel. This is one of the things that impressed me most about Teresita, that she never tired of addressing the Blessed Mother. Her most common way of addressing Mary was "My Mother" or "Dearest Mary." She had familiar and spontaneous conversations with Mary throughout the day. Her prayers to Mary were sincere. While in school, she joined the sodality of Our Lady. Members could be elected to certain offices. On the occasion of an election, she said, "Dearest Mother Mary, today's election means that I must grow in virtue. Help me to edify the girls on my team. Teach me how to treat them with patience, charity, and justice. Since you guide every move of my life, dearest Lady, show me how to use this honor that has come to me only for the purpose of bringing glory to God."[101] Or, "My mother, grant that everyone who looks at me may see you."[102] Or, it may be: "Dear Mother of God, since I cannot adequately thank Our Lord for this precious gift, will you thank Him for me and ask Him to place in my soul the grace I need to love and serve Him alone."[103]

She also had short prayers that we could memorize, like: "Mother most pure, guard my purity."[104] If you pick up the biography of

[100]Tirrell, *Mary Was Her Life*, 18.
[101]Tirrell, *Mary Was Her Life*, 44.
[102]Tirrell, *Mary Was Her Life*, 172.
[103]Tirrell, *Mary Was Her Life*, 136.
[104]Tirrell, *Mary Was Her Life*, 64.

Teresa Quevedo, you will encounter the rich spiritual prayers and her simple conversations with Our Lady.

Another prayer she would often pray to Our Lady asked her to take her hand and lead her: "Mary, my mother, take my hand. Lead me along the narrow path."[105] One way that we ask Mary to take our hand in our devotion is through Marian consecration. One of the earliest prayers that Teresita learned was a simple form of consecration to Our Lady. As a student, she had an earnest desire to join Our Lady's Sodality, a spiritual group that gathered for prayers and retreats throughout the year. She attended one of the retreats and absorbed everything the priest was saying. One of the talks was about Marian consecration. She was naturally drawn to want to make her total consecration. She told the priest how, at her First Communion, she had placed her hand in the hand of Our Lady. Ever since, she had followed wherever Mary led. The priest responded, "The only reply I can make is this, you have been living your own true devotion to Our Lady. Nevertheless, it will please her if you make St. Louis de Montfort's Act of Consecration at Holy Mass tomorrow morning."[106] The priest, looking at the heart of Teresita and moved by her devotion, believed she was ready for such a significant moment in her Marian devotion. The process proposed by St. Louis de Montfort included a thirty-three-day preparation period. This priest waived that preparation and allowed her to make her consecration.

The month of May was always a special month for Teresita because it was Our Lady's month. She would always take up a special act of Marian devotion. During her schooling, she asked the sister to allow her to meditate for fifteen minutes each day. When she

[105] Tirrell, *Mary Was Her Life*, 71.
[106] Tirrell, *Mary Was Her Life*, 66.

would write her family from the convent, she would tell them she was praying for their intentions and offering sacrifices for them to the Blessed Mother. She knew Our Lady would receive them and bring them to her Son.

When reading the life of Teresita, in many ways you can see Thérèse of Lisieux alive in the postulant and novice of the Carmel of Carabanchel. St. Thérèse is known for her "Little Way," and Teresita had one of her own. The little way of Teresita consisted of placing "her soul in Mary's hands, confident that she will offer it to Christ in a manner worthy of Him. Since God will not refuse His mother anything, He will accept her offering and fashion the soul after His, which means that it will 'become perfect as our Heavenly Father is perfect.' "[107] Described another way, she says her little way of confidence is an utter trust in Our Lady. It is being confident that all things come to us from our Holy Mother for our sanctification: "Whenever I begin my meditation, mental prayer, office, or any other spiritual exercise, I unite my soul with Mary's and I say to her: 'Virgin Mother of God, your weak child begs you to turn her distraction into your own holy thoughts. I place all my confidence in you!' Then I go on with my prayer because I am confident that, if I fail, my mother will take over. Thus, God will be praised every moment."[108]

Her little way teaches us to have confidence in Mary. That where we lack, if we offer everything to God through Mary, she will make up for what is lacking. We should approach our prayer to God always with great confidence because Mary, our mother, joins us in our prayer.

Those who knew Teresita witnessed her profound devotion to the Blessed Virgin. They were in awe whenever they saw her pray

[107] Tirrell, *Mary Was Her Life*, 92.
[108] Tirrell, *Mary Was Her Life*, 195.

before a statue of Our Lady.[109] They witnessed how she practiced the virtues of Our Lady.[110] Her Jesuit uncle remarked, "Her desires to please the Blessed Virgin Mary, with whom she enjoyed an intimate relationship, were edifying. Her love for Our Lady surpassed the ordinary love of a devotee of Mary. Something about it was contagious."[111] Her aunts and fellow sisters were inspired by her devotion to Mary, just as we are today, encountering her story perhaps for the very first time. She once said that she wanted to love Our Lady more than others.[112] In my study of holy men and women, I am not sure who I would say has surpassed her in loving the Blessed Virgin.

November 1950 was an important month for Teresita—and the Church. It was announced that Pope Pius XII would officially define the dogma of the Assumption and call for a Holy Year to celebrate. Teresita, who always suspected that her earthly life would be a short one, firmly believed that she would be with Our Lady when the dogma was proclaimed. One time she even remarked, "Can you imagine what heaven will be like when the dogma of the Assumption is declared?"[113]

Sure enough, she died at the age of twenty on Holy Saturday—a day dedicated to Our Lady, to remembering Mary's proximity to the tomb and waiting for the Resurrection of Jesus. She was able to celebrate Easter with the angels of Heaven, who chanted the Regina Caeli. Those who knew Teresita and visited her in the last weeks and days of her life asked her to remember them in prayer and to bring their petitions to Our Lady for them.

[109]Tirrell, *Mary Was Her Life*, 69.
[110]Tirrell, *Mary Was Her Life*, 80.
[111]Tirrell, *Mary Was Her Life*, 170.
[112]Tirrell, *Mary Was Her Life*, 129.
[113]Tirrell, *Mary Was Her Life*, 203.

Her father, on the other hand, did not understand why she was so resigned to dying. He believed she could teach people on earth to love Our Lady more if she was alive. She responded to him, "I do not believe it is God's will for me to teach them here to love His Mother. From her side in Heaven, Papa, I will teach many to love Our Lady with abandon, and to go to Our Lord through her."[114]

How to Love Mary like Sr. Teresa of Jesus Quevedo

• Pray this prayer every day for a week and then decide if you wish to incorporate it into your daily spiritual life: "O sweet Virgin Mary, my Mother, I offer myself today completely to you. I beg you to give my body, eyes, ears, and tongue, my heart and soul to Jesus. I am all yours, holy Mother of God. Watch over me! Amen."

• Address Mary in your conversation throughout the day. Have simple conversations with her. How do you address her? My mother? Dearest Mary?

• Keep track of your spiritual sacrifices and offer them as an oblation to Jesus through Mary.

[114]Tirrell, *Mary Was Her Life*, 238.

Conclusion

You Have a Story

This book has shared the stories of twenty-eight holy men and women who have modeled various ways of being devoted to Mary. They have offered many methods for prayer through devotion, and their words can be inspirational. They all arrived at a devotion to Mary that was personal and unique for them. The reality is that you have a story about Mary, too, whether you realize it or not.

In the blank pages that follow, I'd invite you to briefly write your Mary story. The following questions might be of help:

- What is your earliest memory of the Blessed Mother in your life?
- Has a specific devotion to Mary been influential in your life? Why are you drawn to that form of devotion?
- Have you asked for Mary's prayers and seen the fruit of those prayers as a grace received?
- What attributes of Mary have you admired and can be of assistance to your Christian living?
- Is there a Marian apparition you have gravitated toward or that has touched your life?

Now tell your story and share it with the world.

Sources

Lesson 1: Every Saint Is Devoted to Mary in Some Way — St. Damien of Molokai

Father Pamphile, *Life and Letters of Father Damien: The Apostle of the Lepers* (London: Catholic Truth Society, 1889).

Vital Jourdain, *The Heart of Father Damien* (Milwaukee, WI: Bruce Publishing Company, 1955).

Lesson 2: A Greeting for Mary — St. Francis of Assisi

Regis J. Armstrong, Wayne Hellmann, and William Short, eds., *Francis of Assisi, vol. 1: The Saint: Early Documents* (Hyde Park, NY: New City Press, 1999).

Little Office of the Passion.

Fr. Paschal Yohe, "Virgin Made Church: The Ecclesial-Typical Insight of St. Francis of Assisi," term paper (Mount St. Mary, Emmitsburg, MD, 2011).

Lesson 3: Love Our Lady and Make Her Loved — St. Padre Pio

Br. Francis Mary, "The Madonna in Padre Pio's Life," in *Padre Pio: The Wonder Worker* (New Bedford, MA: Franciscan Friars of the Immaculate, 1999).

"Padre Pio's Love for the Blessed Virgin Mary," Pray, Hope, and Don't Worry, *Padre Pio Newsletter*, no. 75, 1–3, https://padrepiodevotions.org/wp-content/uploads/2018/04/75-Apr2018-SaintPio_Web.pdf.

Lesson 4: Mary Knows Our Suffering—Mother Angelica

Raymond Arroyo, *Mother Angelica: The Remarkable Story of a Nun, Her Nerve, and a Network of Miracles* (New York: Doubleday, 2005).

Raymond Arroyo, *Mother Angelica: Her Grand Silence* (New York: Image Books, 2016).

Mother Angelica, *On Christ and Our Lady* (Irondale, AL: EWTN Publishing, Inc., 2016).

Mother Angelica, *The Prayers and Personal Devotions of Mother Angelica* (New York: Doubleday, 2010).

Lesson 5: Relying on Mary's Prayers—Adele Brise

Sr. M. Dominica, OSF, *The Chapel: Our Lady of Good Help* (Green Bay, WI: The Sisters of St. Francis of Bay Settlement, 1955).

Edward Looney, *Our Lady of Good Help: A Prayer Book for Pilgrims*, (Charlotte, NC: TAN Books, 2019).

Lesson 6: A Childlike Love for Mary—St. Thérèse of Lisieux

St. Thérèse of Lisieux, *Story of a Soul: A Study Edition* (Washington, DC: ICS Publications, 2005).

Lesson 7: Catechesis About Mary Impacted Her Life—St. Kateri Tekakwitha

Lynn Marie Busch, "The Marian Spirituality of Saint Kateri Tekakwitha (1656–1680), in *Marian Studies LXII* (2011): 1–29.

Sources

Lesson 8: Streams of Grace—St. Faustina Kowalska

St. Faustina Kowalska, *Divine Mercy in My Soul* (Stockbridge, MA: Marian Press, 2005).

Lesson 9: Dedicated to and Protected by Mary—Archbishop Fulton J. Sheen

Fulton Sheen, *The World's First Love* (San Francisco: Ignatius Press, 2010).

Fulton Sheen, *The Priest Is Not His Own* (San Francisco: Ignatius Press, 2004).

Personal conversation with Alan Smith.

Lesson 10: A Love for Mary's Many Names—Mother Mary Francis, PCC

Mother Mary Francis, *Cause of Our Joy* (San Francisco: Ignatius Press, 2018).

Archival material received from the Monastery of Our Lady of Guadalupe, Roswell, NM.

Lesson 11: Sincerity in Devotion— Fr. Lukas Etlin, OSB

Rt. Rev. Dr. Norbert Weber, *Father Lukas Etlin, OSB: A Short Biography* (Clyde, MO: Benedictine Convent of Perpetual Adoration, 1931).

Homilies of Fr. Lukas Etlin obtained from the Archives of the Benedictine Sisters in Clyde, MO: Feast of the Annunciation, March 25, 1922; Commemoration of the Annunciation, April 9, 1923; Feast of the Holy Rosary, October 7, 1923; Feast of the Annunciation, March 25, 1924; Feast of the Assumption, August 15, 1925; Feast of the Immaculate Conception, December 8, 1927.

Lesson 12: A New Way to Pray—
St. Ignatius of Loyola

St. Ignatius of Loyola, *The Spiritual Exercises of Saint Ignatius: or Manresa* (Charlotte, NC: TAN Classics, 1999).

Tom Casey, "Mary—How She Made a New Man of Ignatius," https://www.jesuit.ie/blog/tom-casey-sj/may-mary-made-new -man-ignatius/.

Lesson 13: He Preached the Virgin Mother's
Glory—St. Bernard of Clairvaux

St. Bernard of Clairvaux, *Missus Est* homily.

St. Bernard of Clairvaux, *Sermons for the Autumn Season* (Collegeville, MN: Liturgical Press, 2016).

St. Bernard of Clairvaux, *Selected Works* (New York: Paulist Press, 1987).

Lesson 14: Mary Is Our Lifelong
Friend—Francis Cardinal George, OMI

Interviews with Fr. Dan Flens and Margaret Cain.

Chicago New World (archdiocesan newspaper).

Lesson 15: The Goodness of Devotion to
Mary—Blessed Columba Marmion

Columba Marmion, *Christ, The Life of the Soul* (Bethesda: Zaccheus Press, 2005).

Columba Marmion, *Christ, The Ideal of the Priest* (San Francisco: Ignatius Press, 2005).

Rev. David J. Hankus, *Blessed Columba Marmion and the Understanding of the Role of the Blessed Virgin Mary in the Life of a Roman Catholic Priest* (Bloomington, IN: Xlibris Corporation, 2013).

Sources

Lesson 16: A Life of Union with Jesus
and Mary—Fr. Emile Neubert

Fr. Emile Neubert, *Mary and the Priestly Ministry* (New Bedford, MA: Academy of the Immaculate, 2009).

Fr. Emile Neubert, *Mary's Apostolic Mission and Ours* (New Bedford, MA: Academy of the Immaculate, 2011).

Fr. Emil Neubert, *My Ideal: Jesus Son of Mary* (Charlotte, NC: TAN, 1947).

Fr. Emil Neubert, *Queen of Militants* (St. Meinrad, IN: Grail Publications, 1947).

Fr. Emile Neubert, *Life of Union with Mary* (Milwaukee: Bruce, 1959).

Br. John Samaha, "Father Emile Neubert: Our Lady's Dolphin," in *Vocations and Prayer* (July 2013): 23–24.

Paulo Risso, "Emile Neubert: Educator of Saints," https://udayton.edu/imri/mary/e/emile-neubert-educator-of-saints.php.

Lesson 17: The Realness and Relatability
of Mary—Caryll Houselander

Caryll Houselander, *The Reed of God* (Notre Dame, IN: Christian Classics, 2020).

Mary Fiorito, "Who Was Caryll Houselander, and Why Was She Called 'A Divine Eccentric'?," September 25, 2019, https://eppc.org/publication/who-was-caryll-houselander-and-why-was-she-called-a-divine-eccentric/.

Robin Maas, "Caryll Houselander: An Appreciation," https://www.ewtn.com/catholicism/library/caryll-houselander-an-appreciation-10699.

Lesson 18: Lead with Mary—
Pope Francis

Pope Francis, *Ave Maria: The Mystery of a Most Beloved Prayer* (New York: Random House, 2019).

Lesson 19: Challenging Words to Live—Chiara Lubich

Chiara Lubich, *Essential Writings* (Hyde Park, NY: New City Press, 2007).

Chiara Lubich, *Mary: The Transparency of God* (Hyde Park, NY: New City Press, 2003).

Lesson 20: To Think Deeply about Mary—St. Thomas Aquinas

St. Thomas Aquinas, *Summa Theologica.*

Luigi Gambero, *Mary in the Middle Ages* (San Francisco: Ignatius Press, 2005).

Matt Fradd, *Marian Consecration with Aquinas* (Charlotte: TAN Books, 2019).

Lesson 21: Mary Was with Her— St.
Mariam of Jesus Crucified

Fr. Amedee Brunot, *Mariam the Little Arab* (Jerusalem: Latin Patriarchate Printing Press, 2013).

Mariam of Jesus Crucified, *Thoughts* (Jerusalem: Franciscan Printing Press, 1997).

Sr. Emmanuel Maillard, *Maryam of Bethlehem: The Little Arab* (n.p.: Children of Medjugorje, 2011).

Lesson 22: The Rosary Is Meant for Family
Prayer—Fr. Patrick Peyton

Patrick Peyton, *All for Her: The Autobiography of Father Patrick Peyton, CSC* (Notre Dame, IN: Ave Maria Press, 2018).

Sources

Lesson 23: The Use of Imaginative Prayer When Receiving Holy Communion — Fr. Daniel Lord, SJ

Daniel Lord, *The Song of the Rosary* (St. Louis, MO: Eucharistic Crusade of the Knights and Handmaids of the Blessed Sacrament, 1953).

Daniel Lord, *Christ in Me: Meditations after Holy Communion* (St. Louis, MO: Queen's Work, 1934).

Daniel Lord, *Our Lady in the Modern World* (St. Louis, MO: Queen's Work, 1940).

Lesson 24: A Simple Approach to Marian Devotion — Blessed Solanus Casey

Michael Crosby, *Thank God Ahead of Time: The Life and Spirituality of Solanus Casey* (Cincinnati, OH: Franciscan Media, 2017).

Lesson 25: What Mary's Feasts Mean for Us — St. Francis de Sales

St. Francis de Sales, *On Our Lady: The Sermons of St. Francis de Sales* (Charlotte, NC: TAN Books, 2013).

Lesson 26: Give Your Life to Mary — Venerable Aloysius Schwartz

Kevin Wells, *Priest and Beggar: The Heroic Life of Venerable Aloysius Schwartz* (San Francisco: Ignatius Press, 2021).

Lesson 27: Be Joyful with Mary — Sr. Clare Crockett

Sr. Kristen Gardner, *Sr. Clare Crockett: Alone with Christ Alone* (New Hope, KY: New Hope Publications, 2021).

"All or Nothing: Sr. Clare Crockett," HM Television, documentary, 2018, https://www.youtube.com/watch?v=-0LKZm2BqZo&t=24s.

Sr. Clare Website: https://www.sisterclare.com/en/.

Lesson 28: The Little Way of Confidence in
Mary—Sr. Teresa of Jesus Quevedo

Sr. Mary Pierre Tirrell, RSM, *Mary Was Her Life: The Story of a Nun, Sister Maria Teresa Quevedo 1930–1950* (n.p.: Barakaldo Books, 2020).

Meg Hunter-Kilmer, *Pray for Us: 75 Saints Who Sinned, Suffered, and Struggled on Their Way to Holiness* (Notre Dame, IN: Ave Maria Press, 2021).

Acknowledgments

This book has been the fruit of the years of my study of and devotion to the Blessed Virgin Mary. I am grateful for those in my life who have witnessed their love for Mary. It has been influential for me. The Diocese of Green Bay afforded me the opportunity to study theology, which allowed me to be introduced to many of these figures. My time in seminary at Conception Seminary College and Mundelein Seminary also afforded me plenty of opportunities to deepen my love for Mary. My membership in the Mariological Society of America has also allowed me to research more extensively certain individuals included in this book. I'm grateful for the MSA's invitation to present and publish in their journal, *Marian Studies*.

This book has been a long time coming. When I started my podcast, *How They Love Mary*, I knew I wanted to write a book of the same title in the future. I reached out to several publishers, and the timing was never right for them. Three years in the making, this book has taken a different shape than I originally conceived. Sometimes time makes things better. I'm grateful to Sophia Institute Press for believing in the book after my second or third proposal and for allowing what I consider my greatest contribution to Marian theology to come to life. For those who talked to me along the way and helped me, thank you for your words of counsel and inspiration. Nancy Lind, professor emeritus of Political Science at Illinois State University and a seasonal parishioner of mine has enjoyed proofing my manuscripts for typos and giving helpful suggestions for content before submission, and she assisted me in this way with this book.

A handful of people were instrumental in supplementing my reading and research. My longtime friend Mike Stark filmed a documentary about Cardinal George. During that time, he asked Cardinal George's sister Margaret Cain a few questions about the Cardinal's Marian devotion. Fr. Dan Flens also offered a few insights in an e-mail exchange.

The Poor Clare Colettines in Roswell, New Mexico, sent me a plethora of newsletters and writings of Mother Mary Francis for my reading and research.

The Benedictine Sisters in Clyde, Missouri, referred me to the biography of Fr. Lukas Etlin, and they were kind enough to send me several of Fr. Lukas Etlin's homilies about the Blessed Virgin and her feast days.

Fr. Paschal, MFVA, sent me a copy of his term paper about St. Francis and Mary that was influential in my writing of Lesson Two.

Alan Smith has a profound devotion to Ven. Fulton Sheen and was kind enough to record a video for me reflecting Sheen's Marian devotion.

Fr. Joe Laramie, SJ, directed me to a Marian reference in St. Ignatius's *Spiritual Exercises* that I was unable to find myself.

All praise and thanks belong to God, who inspired my great love for the Mother of God. I am grateful for the working of the Trinity and for the prayers of our Heavenly Mother, who helped me bring this work to completion.

Little Office of the Blessed Virgin Mary, Morning Prayer

Saturday

God, come to my assistance.

—Lord, make haste to help me

Glory to the Father and to the Son and to the Holy Spirit
as it was in the beginning, is now, and will be forever. Amen.

Hymn

Hail, holy Queen of the Heavens.
Hail, holy Queen of the Angels.
Hail, Root of Jesse.
Hail, Gate of Heaven.
By you the Light has entered the world.
Rejoice, glorious Virgin,
Beautiful among all women.
Hail, radiant Splendor,
Intercede with Christ for us.

Melody: Hail Holy Queen.
Music: Lucien Deiss, CSSp, 1965
Text: Lucien Deiss, CSSp, 1965

How They Love Mary

 Or:

Holy Mary,
my Queen and sovereign Lady,
I give you myself,
trusting in your fidelity and your protection.

I surrender myself entirely
to your motherly tenderness,
my body, my soul,
all that I am,
all that I possess,
for the whole of this day,
for every moment of my life,
and especially at the hour of my death.

I entrust to you once more
all my hopes, all my consolations,
all my anxieties, all my troubles,
my life, my dying breath,
so that by your prayers and merits,
I may have, in all I do, one only goal,
your good pleasure and the holy will of your Son.

St. Pere Raphael (seventeenth century)

Psalmody

Ant. 1: Blessed are you, O Mary, for the world's salvation came forth through you; now in glory, you rejoice for ever with the Lord.

or: Arise, O Virgin Queen, you are for ever worthy of our praise; take your place in the glorious dwelling place of our eternal King.

Psalm 92

Praise of God the Creator
Sing in praise of Christ's redeeming work. (St. Athanasius)

It is good to give thanks to the Lord,
to make music to your name, O Most High,
to proclaim your love in the morning
and your truth in the watches of the night,
on the ten-stringed lyre and the lute,
with the murmuring sound of the harp.

Your deeds, O Lord, have made me glad;
for the work of your hands I shout with joy.
O Lord, how great are your works!
How deep are your designs!
The foolish man cannot know this
and the fool cannot understand.

Though the wicked spring up like grass
and all who do evil thrive,
they are doomed to be eternally destroyed.
But you, Lord, are eternally on high.
See how your enemies perish;
all doers of evil are scattered.

To me you give the wild ox's strength;
you anoint me with the purest oil.
My eyes looked in triumph on my foes;
my ears heard gladly of their fall.
The just will flourish like the palm tree
and grow like a Lebanon cedar.

How They Love Mary

Planted in the house of the Lord
they will flourish in the courts of our God,
still bearing fruit when they are old,
still full of sap, still green,
to proclaim that the Lord is just.
In him, my rock, there is no wrong.

Ant. 2: The Virgin Mary is exalted above the choirs of angels; let
all believers rejoice and bless the Lord.

✢ Or: The Lord has chosen her, his loved one from the beginning.
He has taken her to live with him.

Canticle: Ezekiel 36:24–28
The Lord will renew his people
*They will be his own people, and God himself will be with them, their
own God.* (Revelation 21:3)

I will take you away from among the nations,
gather you from all the foreign lands,
and bring you back to your own land.

I will sprinkle clean water upon you
to cleanse you from all your impurities,
and from all your idols I will cleanse you.

I will give you a new heart
and place a new spirit within you,
taking from your bodies your stony hearts
and giving you natural hearts.

I will put my spirit within you
and make you live by my statutes,
careful to observe my decrees.

You shall live in the land I gave your fathers;
you shall be my people,
and I will be your God.

Ant. 3: The Lord has made you so glorious that your praise will
never cease to resound among men.

✝ Or: Glorious things are said of you, O Virgin Mary.

Psalm 8

The majesty of the Lord and man's dignity
The Father gave Christ lordship of creation (Ephesians 1:22)

How great is your name, O Lord our God,
through all the earth!

Your majesty is praised above the heavens;
on the lips of children and of babes
you have found praise to foil your enemy,
to silence the foe and the rebel.

When I see the heavens, the work of your hands,
the moon and the stars which you arranged,
what is man that you should keep him in mind,
mortal man that you care for him?

Yet you have made him little less than a god;
with glory and honor you crowned him,
gave him power over the works of your hands,
put all things under his feet.

All of them, sheep and cattle,
yes, even the savage beasts,
birds of the air, and fish
that make their way through the waters.

How great is your name, O Lord our God
through all the earth!

First Reading: See Isaiah 61:10

I rejoice heartily in the Lord,
in my God is the joy of my soul;
For he has clothed me with a robe of salvation,
and wrapped me in a mantle of justice,
like a bride bedecked with her jewels.

✻ Or: Revelation 12:1

A great sign appeared in the sky, a woman clothed with the sun,
with the moon under her feet, and on her head a crown of twelve
stars.

✝ Or: Judith 13:17-20

All the people were greatly astonished. They bowed down and
worshiped God, saying with one accord, "Blessed are you, our
God, who today have brought to nought the enemies of your
people."

Then Uzziah said to her: "Blessed are you, daughter, by the
Most High God, above all the women on earth; and blessed
be the Lord God, the creator of heaven and earth, who guided
your blow at the head of the chief of our enemies. Your deed
of hope will never be forgotten by those who tell of the might
of God.

"May God make this redound to your everlasting honor, re-
warding you with blessings, because you risked your life when
your people were being oppressed, and you averted our disaster,
walking uprightly before our God." And all the people answered,
"Amen! Amen!"

Second Reading

From a letter by Paschasius Radbert, abbot
(Letter *Cogito me* 20–23,26,28: PL 30, 122,42)

Mary is taken from earth

Today the glorious, ever-virgin Mary ascends to heaven. I urge you to rejoice, for, if I may so put it, she has been raised up in an ineffable way to be with Christ who reigns for ever. The Queen of the world is today taken from the earth and from this present evil time. I say again: rejoice, because she who is sure of her imperishable glory has reached the palace of heaven.

Exult, I say, and rejoice, and let the whole world rejoice, because this day Salvation has drawn nearer for us all....

"Hail, Mary, full of grace; the Lord is with thee; blessed art thou amongst women." It was fitting that the Virgin should be given such gifts and be full of grace, since she has bestowed glory on heaven and has brought God and peace to the earth, faith to pagans, an end to vice, order to life, and discipline to morals.

And it was right that an angel be sent to the Virgin, because virginity always means kinship with the angels....

"Rejoice," the angel says, "for you are full of grace." Yes, full! For while a share of grace was given to others, the undiminished fullness of grace was poured into Mary.

Responsory

The Virgin Mary was taken up to heaven.
—The Virgin Mary was taken up to heaven.
For all eternity she shares the victory of Christ.
—The Virgin Mary was taken up to heaven.
Glory to the Father and to the Son and to the Holy Spirit.
—The Virgin Mary was taken up to heaven.

OR ➔

How They Love Mary

✳ Or:

After the birth of your son, you remained a virgin.
—After the birth of your son, you remained a virgin.
Mother of God, intercede for us;
—you remained a virgin.
Glory to the Father and to the Son and to the Holy Spirit.
—After the birth of your son, you remained a virgin.

Canticle of Zechariah: Luke 1:68–79

Ant.: This daughter of Jerusalem is lovely and beautiful as she ascends to heaven like the rising sun at daybreak.

The Messiah and his forerunner

Blessed be the Lord, the God of Israel;
he has come to his people and set them free.
He has raised up for us a mighty savior,
born of the house of his servant David.
Through his holy prophets he promised of old,
that he would save us from our enemies,
from the hands of all who hate us.
He promised to show mercy to our fathers
and to remember his holy covenant.
This was the oath he swore to our father Abraham,
to set us free from the hands of our enemies,
free to worship him without fear,
holy and righteous in his sight
all the days of our life.
You, my child, shall be called the prophet of the Most High,
for you will go before the Lord to prepare his way,
To give his people knowledge of salvation
by the forgiveness of their sins.

In the tender compassion of our God
the dawn from on high shall break upon us,
to shine on those who dwell in darkness and the shadow
of death,
and to guide our feet into the way of peace.
Glory to the Father, and to the Son, and to the Holy Spirit:
as it was in the beginning, is now, and will be for ever. Amen.

Intercessions

Let us glorify our Savior, who chose the Virgin Mary for his
mother. Let us ask him:
May your mother intercede for us, Lord.

Eternal Word, you chose Mary as the uncorrupted ark of your
dwelling place,
—free us from the corruption of sin.

You are our redeemer, who made the immaculate Virgin Mary
your purest home and the sanctuary of the Holy Spirit,
—make us temples of your Spirit for ever.

King of kings, you lifted up your mother, body and soul, into
heaven,
—help us to fix our thoughts on things above.

Lord of heaven and earth, you crowned Mary and set her at
your right hand as queen,
—make us worthy to share this glory.

Our Father ...

Concluding Prayer

All-powerful and ever-living God,
you raised the sinless Virgin Mary,

How They Love Mary

mother of your Son,
body and soul to the glory of heaven.
May we see heaven as our final goal
and come to share her glory.

We ask this through our Lord Jesus Christ, your Son,
who lives and reigns with you and the Holy Spirit,
one God, for ever and ever.

May the Lord bless us,
protect us from evil
and bring us to everlasting life.
—Amen.

Little Office of the Blessed Virgin Mary, Evening Prayer

Saturday

God, come to my assistance.
— Lord, make haste to help me

Glory to the Father and to the Son and to the Holy Spirit
as it was in the beginning, is now, and will be forever. Amen.

Hymn

Praise to Mary, Heaven's Gate,
Guiding Star of Christians' way,
Mother of our Lord and King,
Light and hope to souls astray.

When you heard the call of God
Choosing to fulfill his plan,
By your perfect act of love
Hope was born in fallen man.

Help us to amend our ways,
Halt the devil's strong attack,

Q R

How They Love Mary

Walk with us the narrow path,
Beg for us the grace we lack.

Mary, show your motherhood,
Bring your children's prayers to Christ,
Christ, your son, who ransomed man,
Who, for us, was sacrificed.

Virgin chosen, singly blest,
Ever faithful to God's call,
Guide us in this earthy life,
Guard us lest, deceived, we fall.

Mary, help us live our faith
So that we may see your son;
Join our humble prayers to yours,
Till life's ceaseless war is won.

Praise the Father, praise the Son,
Praise the holy Paraclete;
Offer all through Mary's hands,
Let her make our prayers complete.

Melody: Gott sei dank 77.77
Music: Freylinghausen's, 1670–1739
Text: V.S.S. Coles, 1845–1929

⚹ Or:

My Lady, my refuge,
life and help,
my armor and my boast,
my hope and my strength,
grant that I may enjoy
the ineffable, inconceivable gifts of your Son,

your God and our God,
in the heavenly kingdom.
For I know surely
that you have power to do as you will,
since you are Mother of the Most High.
Therefore, Lady Most Pure,
I beg you
that I may not be disappointed in my expectations
but may obtain them, O spouse of God,
who bore him who is the expectation of all:
Our Lord Jesus Christ,
true God and Master of all things,
visible and invisible,
to whom belongs all glory, honor, and respect,
now and always and through endless ages. Amen.

(Saint Germanius of Constantinople [ca. 634-730])

Psalmody

Ant. 1: Mary has been taken up to heaven; the angels rejoice. They bless the Lord and sing his praises.

✝ Or: Christ ascended into heaven and prepared an everlasting place for his immaculate Mother.

Psalm 122

Holy city Jerusalem
You have come to Mount Zion, the city of the living God, heavenly Jerusalem. (Hebrews 12:22)

I rejoiced when I heard them say:
Let us go to God's house.

How They Love Mary

And now our feet are standing
within your gates, O Jerusalem.

Jerusalem is built as a city
strongly compact.
It is there that the tribes go up,
the tribes of the Lord.

For Israel's law it is,
there to praise the Lord's name.
There were set the thrones of judgment
of the house of David.

For the peace of Jerusalem pray:
Peace be to your homes!

For love of my brethren and friends
I say: Peace upon you.
For love of the house of the Lord
I will ask for your good.

Ant. 2: The Virgin Mary was taken up to the heavenly bridal
chamber where the King of kings is seated on a heavenly throne.

✗ Or: Through Eve the gates of heaven were closed to all mankind: through the Virgin Mother they were opened wide again.

Psalm 130

A cry from the depths
He himself will save his people from their sins (Matthew 1:21).

Out of the depths I cry to you, O Lord,
Lord, hear my voice!
O let your ears be attentive
to the voice of my pleading.

If you, O Lord, should mark our guilt,
Lord, who would survive?
But with you is found forgiveness:
for this we revere you.

My soul is waiting for the Lord.
I count on his word.
My soul is longing for the Lord
more than watchman for daybreak.
(Let the watchman count on daybreak
and Israel on the Lord.)

Because with the Lord there is mercy
and fullness of redemption,
Israel indeed he will redeem
from all its iniquity.

Ant. 3: We share the fruit of life through you, O daughter blessed
by the Lord.

✝ Or: The Virgin Mary has been exalted above all the heavens; come,
let all men glorify Christ the King, whose kingdom will endure
for ever.

Canticle: Philippians 2:6–11
Christ, God's holy servant

Though he was in the form of God,
Jesus did not deem equality with God
something to be grasped at.

Rather, he emptied himself
and took the form of a slave,
being born in the likeness of men.

He was known to be of human estate
and it was thus that he humbled himself,
obediently accepting even death,
death on a cross!

Because of this,
God highly exalted him
and bestowed on him the name
above every other name,

So that at Jesus' name
every knee must bend
in the heavens, on the earth,
and under the earth,
and every tongue proclaim
to the glory of God the Father:
JESUS CHRIST IS LORD!

First Reading: 1 Corinthians 15:22–23

Just as in Adam all die, so too in Christ shall all be brought to life, but each one in proper order: Christ the firstfruits; then, at his coming, those who belong to Christ.

✝ Or: Judith 13:17b, 18a

Blessed are you, our God, who today have brought to nought the enemies of your people. Blessed are you, daughter, by the Most High God, above all the women on earth.

✝ Or: Revelation 12:1

A great sign appeared in the sky, a woman clothed with the sun, with the moon under her feet, and on her head a crown of twelve stars.

℣ Or: Romans 5:12–21

Just as through one person sin entered the world, and through sin, death, and thus death came to all, inasmuch as all sinned—for up to the time of the law, sin was in the world, though sin is not accounted when there is no law. But death reigned from Adam to Moses, even over those who did not sin after the pattern of the trespass of Adam, who is the type of the one who was to come.

But the gift is not like the transgression. For if by that one person's transgression the many died, how much more did the grace of God and the gracious gift of the one person Jesus Christ overflow for the many. And the gift is not like the result of the one person's sinning. For after one sin there was the judgment that brought condemnation; but the gift, after many transgressions, brought acquittal. For if, by the transgression of one person, death came to reign through that one, how much more will those who receive the abundance of grace and of the gift of justification come to reign in life through the one person Jesus Christ. In conclusion, just as through one transgression condemnation came upon all, so through one righteous act acquittal and life came to all. For just as through the disobedience of one person the many were made sinners, so through the obedience of one the many will be made righteous. The law entered in so that transgression might increase but, where sin increased, grace overflowed all the more, so that, as sin reigned in death, grace also might reign through justification for eternal life through Jesus Christ our Lord.

How They Love Mary

Second Reading
From a homily on the falling asleep of the Blessed Virgin Mary
by Saint Germanus of Constantinople, bishop (*In Dormitionem
B. Mariae* I: PG 98, 345–348)

The Assumption of Mary
Truly, yes truly, and again I shall say in thanksgiving: even though
you have left us, you have not deserted the Christian race. You
who are like incorruptible life have not abandoned our mortal
world, but, on the contrary, you draw near to those who call upon
your name. You are found by those who faithfully seek you. And
these visions indicate a living and continually active spirit and an
everlasting body. For how could dissolution of the body return
you to dust and ashes, you who delivered the human race from
the destruction of death through the incarnation of your Son?

Indeed, you left our earth to prove that the mystery of the awe-
inspiring incarnation was really fulfilled. The fact that you waited
for the natural end of human life would convince the world that
the God who was born of you came into being also as perfect
man, the Son of a true Mother, who was subject to the laws and
constraints of nature, by divine decree and the requirement of an
earthly lifetime. As one who possessed a human body you could
not escape death, the common fate of humanity.

Thus, even your Son, though God of all things, even he, through
sharing, so to speak, the mortality of all our race, "tasted" a similar
bodily "death." It was clearly in the same way as he made his own
life-giving tomb that he made your sepulcher wonderful also, as the
tomb of your falling asleep, a tomb which received life; therefore
both tombs really received your bodies, but could in no way affect
them with corruption. For nor could you, as the vessel which
contained God, waste away to dust in the destruction of death.

For since he who humbled himself in you was God from beginning and eternal life, so the Mother of Life was to share the dwelling of Life, to accept her death like a sleep and consent to her translation like a waking, as the Mother of Life. For just as a child seeks and longs for its own mother, and the mother loves to spend her time with her child, so it was right that you, with your maternal love for your Son and God, should return to him. And it was right too that God, preserving a Son's love for you, should make his companionship with you into a perpetual association.

In this way, then, you suffered the death of finite beings and the translation to the immortal way of life of eternal beings where God dwells; and because you are his companion, Mother of God, you do not abandon your life with him.

✝ Or:

From the Apostolic Constitution *Munificentissimus Deus* by Pope Pius XII (AAS 42 [1950], 760–762,767–769)

Your body is holy and excelling in splendor

The august Mother of God was mysteriously united from all eternity with Jesus Christ in one and the same decree of predestination, immaculate in her conception, a virgin inviolate in her divine motherhood, the wholehearted companion of the divine Redeemer who won complete victory over sin and its consequences.

Thus, she gained at last the supreme crown of her privileges—to be preserved immune from the corruption of the tomb, and like her Son, when death had been conquered, to be carried up body and soul to the exalted glory of heaven, there to sit in splendor at the right hand of her Son, the immortal King of the ages.

How They Love Mary

Responsory

The Virgin Mary is exalted above the choirs of angels.
—The Virgin Mary is exalted above the choirs of angels.
Blessed is the Lord who has raised her up.
—Above the choirs of the angels.
Glory to the Father, and to the Son and to the Holy Spirit
—The Virgin Mary is exalted above the choirs of angels.

✗ Or:

As Mary is taken up to heaven,
the angels of God rejoice.
—As Mary is taken up to heaven,
the angels of God rejoice.
They worship the Lord and sing his praises;
—The angels of God rejoice.
Glory be to the Father and to the Son, and to the Holy Spirit.
—As Mary is taken up to heaven,
the angels of God rejoice.

Canticle of Mary: Luke 1:46–55

Ant: Today the Virgin Mary was taken up to heaven; rejoice, for
she reigns with Christ for ever.

✗ Or: All generations will call me blessed; the Almighty has done
great things for me.

My soul rejoices in the Lord.
My soul proclaims the greatness of the Lord,
my spirit rejoices in God my Savior;
for he has looked with favor on his lowly servant.
From this day all generations will call me blessed:
the Almighty has done great things for me,
and holy is his Name.

He has mercy on those who fear him
in every generation.
He has shown the strength of his arm,
he has scattered the proud in their conceit.
He has cast down the mighty from their thrones,
and has lifted up the lowly.
He has filled the hungry with good things,
and the rich he has sent away empty.
He has come to the help of his servant Israel,
for he has remembered his promise of mercy,
The promise he made to our fathers,
to Abraham and his children for ever.
Glory to the Father, and to the Son, and to the Holy Spirit:
as it was in the beginning, is now, and will be for ever. Amen.

Intercessions

Let us praise God, our almighty Father, who wished that Mary, his
Son's mother, be celebrated by each generation. Now in need we ask:

Mary, full of grace, intercede for us.
O God, worker of miracles, you made the immaculate Virgin
Mary share, body and soul, in your Son's glory in heaven,
—direct the hearts of your children to that same glory.
You made Mary our mother. Through her intercession grant
strength to the weak, comfort to the sorrowing, pardon to sinners,
—Salvation and peace to all.
You made Mary full of grace,
—grant all men the joyful abundance of your grace.
Make your Church of one mind and one heart in love,
—and help all those who believe to be one in prayer with Mary,
the mother of Jesus.

How They Love Mary

You crowned Mary queen of heaven,
— may all the dead rejoice in your kingdom with the saints for
ever.
Our Father ...

Concluding Prayer

All-powerful and everliving God,
you raised the sinless Virgin Mary,
mother of your Son,
body and soul to the glory of heaven.
May we see heaven as our final goal
and come to share her glory.
May the Lord bless us,
protect us from evil
and bring us to everlasting life.
— Amen.

Common Marian Prayers

The Angelus

The Angel of the Lord declared to Mary:
And she conceived of the Holy Spirit.

Hail Mary, full of grace, the Lord is with thee; blessed art thou among women and blessed is the fruit of thy womb, Jesus. Holy Mary, Mother of God, pray for us sinners, now and at the hour of our death. Amen.

Behold the handmaid of the Lord:
Be it done unto me according to Thy word.

Hail Mary ...

And the Word was made Flesh:
And dwelt among us.
Hail Mary ...

Pray for us, O Holy Mother of God,
that we may be made worthy of the promises of Christ.

Let us pray: Pour forth, we beseech Thee, O Lord, Thy grace into our hearts; that we, to whom the incarnation of Christ, Thy Son, was made known by the message of an angel, may by His Passion and Cross be brought to the glory of His Resurrection, through the same Christ Our Lord. Amen.

The Memorare

Remember, O most gracious Virgin Mary, that never was it known that anyone who fled to thy protection, implored thy help, or sought thy intercession, was left unaided. Inspired by this confidence, I fly unto thee, O Virgin of virgins, my Mother. To thee do I come; before thee I stand, sinful and sorrowful. O Mother of the Word Incarnate, despise not my petitions, but in thy mercy, hear and answer me.

Marian Litanies

Litany of Loreto

V. Lord have mercy.

R. Christ have mercy.

V. Lord have mercy.

V. Christ hear us.

R. Christ graciously hear us.

God the Father of heaven, *have mercy on us.*

God the Son, Redeemer of the world, *have mercy on us.*

God the Holy Spirit, *have mercy on us.*

Holy Trinity, one God, *have mercy on us.*

Holy Mary, *pray for us.*

Holy Mother of God, *pray for us.*

Holy Virgin of virgins, *pray for us.*

Mother of Christ, *pray for us.*

Mother of the Church, *pray for us.*

Mother of Mercy, *pray for us.*

Mother of divine grace, *pray for us.*

Mother of Hope, *pray for us.*

Mother most pure, *pray for us.*

How They Love Mary

Mother most chaste, *pray for us.*
Mother inviolate, *pray for us.*
Mother undefiled, *pray for us.*
Mother most amiable, *pray for us.*
Mother admirable, *pray for us.*
Mother of good counsel, *pray for us.*
Mother of our Creator, *pray for us.*
Mother of our Savior, *pray for us.*
Virgin most prudent, *pray for us.*
Virgin most venerable, *pray for us.*
Virgin most renowned, *pray for us.*
Virgin most powerful, *pray for us.*
Virgin most merciful, *pray for us.*
Virgin most faithful, *pray for us.*
Mirror of justice, *pray for us.*
Seat of wisdom, *pray for us.*
Cause of our joy, *pray for us.*
Spiritual vessel, *pray for us.*
Vessel of honor, *pray for us.*
Singular vessel of devotion, *pray for us.*
Mystical rose, *pray for us.*
Tower of David, *pray for us.*
Tower of ivory, *pray for us.*
House of gold, *pray for us.*
Ark of the covenant, *pray for us.*
Gate of heaven, *pray for us.*
Morning star, *pray for us.*
Health of the sick, *pray for us.*
Refuge of sinners, *pray for us.*
Solace of Migrants, *pray for us.*
Comfort of the afflicted, *pray for us.*

Help of Christians, *pray for us.*
Queen of Angels, *pray for us.*
Queen of Patriarchs, *pray for us.*
Queen of Prophets, *pray for us.*
Queen of Apostles, *pray for us.*
Queen of Martyrs, *pray for us.*
Queen of Confessors, *pray for us.*
Queen of Virgins, *pray for us.*
Queen of all Saints, *pray for us.*
Queen conceived without original sin, *pray for us.*
Queen assumed into Heaven, *pray for us.*
Queen of the most Holy Rosary, *pray for us.*
Queen of families, *pray for us.*
Queen of peace, *pray for us.*

V. Lamb of God, Who takest away the sins of the world,
R. Spare us, O Lord.
V. Lamb of God, Who takest away the sins of the world,
R. Graciously hear us, O Lord.
V. Lamb of God, Who takest away the sins of the world,
R. Have mercy on us.
V. Pray for us, O holy Mother of God.
R. That we may be made worthy of the promises of Christ.

Let us pray. Grant, we beseech Thee, O Lord God, that we thy servants may enjoy perpetual health of mind and body, and by the glorious intercession of blessed Mary, ever Virgin, may be freed from present sorrow, and rejoice in eternal happiness. Through Christ our Lord.

R. Amen.

How They Love Mary

Litany of Our Lady of Good Help

V. Lord, have mercy. R. Lord have mercy.
V. Christ, have mercy. R. Christ have mercy.
V. Lord, have mercy. R. Christ have mercy.
V. Christ, hear us.
R. Christ, graciously hear us.

God the Father of Heaven, have mercy on us.
God the Son, Redeemer of the world, have mercy on us.
God the Holy Spirit, have mercy on us.
Holy Trinity, one God, have mercy on us.

Holy Mary, *pray for us.*
Holy Mother of God, *pray for us.*
Queen of Heaven, *pray for us.*
Star of the Sea, *pray for us.*
Comforter of the Afflicted, *pray for us.*
Health of the Sick, *pray for us.*
Refuge of Sinners, *pray for us.*
Star of the New Evangelization, *pray for us.*
Our Lady of Good Help, *pray for us.*

In times of temptation, *Mary, help us.*
In times of sickness, *Mary, help us.*
In times of sorrow, *Mary, help us.*
In times of confusion, *Mary, help us.*
In times of persecution, *Mary, help us.*
In times of failure, *Mary, help us.*
In times of betrayal, *Mary, help us.*
In times of weakness, *Mary, help us.*
In times of discernment, *Mary, help us.*
In times of war, *Mary, help us.*

For those who are unemployed, *Mary, help them.*
For those who are homeless, *Mary, help them.*
For those who struggle to make ends meet, *Mary, help them.*
For those in troubled marriages, *Mary, help them.*
For those contemplating abortion, *Mary, help them.*
For those contemplating suicide, *Mary, help them.*
For those who are sick, *Mary, help them.*
For those suffering with physical handicaps, *Mary, help them.*
For those unable to conceive, *Mary, help them.*
For those trapped in a life of sin, *Mary, help them.*
For those who suffer from addictions, *Mary, help them.*
For those near death, *Mary, help them.*
For those who do not believe in God, *Mary, help them.*
For those who have rejected God's commandments, *Mary, help them.*
For fallen away Catholics, *Mary, help them.*
For those who need our prayers, *Mary, help them.*
For the immigrant, *Mary, help them.*
For the poor souls in purgatory, *Mary, help them.*
For teachers and catechists, *Mary, help them.*
For Catholic schools and universities, *Mary, help them.*
For Catholic parishes, *Mary, help them.*
For bishops, priests, deacons, and seminarians, *Mary, help them.*
For consecrated religious, *Mary, help them.*
For missionaries, *Mary, help them.*
For families, *Mary, help them.*

V. Lamb of God, who takes away the sins of the world,
R. Spare us, O Lord.
V. Lamb of God, who takes away the sins of the world,
R. Graciously hear us, O Lord.
V. Lamb of God, who takes away the sins of the world,
R. Have mercy on us.

V. Pray for us, O holy Mother of God.

R. That we may be made worthy of the promises of Christ.

Let us pray: Grant O God, through the intercession and mediation of Our Lady of Good Help, all the graces we need to live a life in accordance with your will. Come to the help of your servants who are in need of heavenly assistance. Incline your ear to the prayers offered by them through the intercession of the Queen of Heaven, through Christ our Lord. Amen.

Litany of Our Lady of Banneux

Blessed Virgin of the Poor,
Lead us to Jesus, Source of grace.
Blessed Virgin of the Poor,
Save all nations.
Blessed Virgin of the Poor,
Relieve the sick.
Blessed Virgin of the Poor,
Alleviate suffering.
Blessed Virgin of the Poor,
Pray for each one of us.
Blessed Virgin of the Poor,
We believe in thee.
Blessed Virgin of the Poor,
Believe in us.
Blessed Virgin of the Poor,
We will pray hard.
Blessed Virgin of the Poor,
Bless us.
Blessed Virgin of the Poor, Mother of the Saviour, Mother of God,
We thank thee.

Let us pray: Our Lady of Banneux, Mother of Our Saviour, Mother of God, Virgin of the Poor, since thou hast promised to believe in us if we believe in thee, I put all my trust in thee. Deign to listen to the prayers that thou hast asked be addressed to thee; have pity on all our spiritual and temporal miseries. Restore to sinners the treasure of faith, and give to the poor their daily bread. Deign to relieve suffering, to heal the sick and to pray for us, so that thus through thy intercession, the reign of Christ the King may extend over all nations. R. Amen.

Marian Prayer of St. Thomas Aquinas

O most blessed and sweet Virgin Mary,
Mother of God, filled with all tenderness,
Daughter of the most high King,
Lady of the Angels,
Mother of all the faithful,
On this day and all the days of my life
I entrust to your merciful heart my body and my soul,
all my acts, thoughts, choices,
desires, words, deeds,
my entire life and death,
So that, with your assistance,
all may be ordered to the good
according to the will of your beloved Son, our Lord
    Jesus Christ....
From your beloved Son...
request for me the grace to resist firmly
the temptations of the world, the flesh and the
    devil....
My most holy Lady,
I also beseech you to obtain for me

How They Love Mary

true obedience and true humility of heart
So that I may recognize myself truly
as a sinner—wretched and weak—and powerless,
without the grace and help of my Creator
and without your holy prayers....
Obtain for me as well,
O most sweet Lady,
true charity with which from the depths of my heart
I may love your most holy Son, our Lord Jesus Christ,
and, after Him,
love you above all other things....
Grant, O Queen of Heaven,
that ever in my heart
I may have fear and love alike
for your most sweet Son....
I pray also that, at the end of my life,
you, Mother without compare,
Gate of Heaven and Advocate of sinners....
will protect me with your great piety and mercy....
and obtain for me, through the blessed and glorious
      Passion of your Son
and through your own intercession,
received in hope, the forgiveness of all my sins.
When I die in your love and His love,
may you direct me
into the way of salvation and blessedness. Amen.[115]

---

[115] "Prayer of St. Thomas Aquinas to the Blessed Virgin," in St.
Thomas Aquinas, *Devoutly I Adore Thee*, trans. and ed. Robert
Anderson and Johann Moser (Manchester, NH: Sophia Institute
Press, 1993), 21–31.

About the Author

Fr. Edward Looney was ordained a priest for the Diocese of Green Bay in June 2015 and is an internationally recognized Marian theologian, writer, speaker, and radio personality. He is a member of the Mariological Society of America and, since 2016, has served on its administrative council. He is the best-selling author of *A Heart Like Mary's* (Ave Maria Press), *A Rosary Litany* (Our Sunday Visitor), and *A Lenten Journey with Mother Mary* (Sophia Institute Press). His writings appear in many print publications and online at *Catholic Exchange* and Aleteia. He also hosts the podcast *How They Love Mary*. You can follow him on social media at @FrEdwardLooney.

Sophia Institute

Sophia Institute is a nonprofit institution that seeks to nurture the spiritual, moral, and cultural life of souls and to spread the gospel of Christ in conformity with the authentic teachings of the Roman Catholic Church.

Sophia Institute Press fulfills this mission by offering translations, reprints, and new publications that afford readers a rich source of the enduring wisdom of mankind.

Sophia Institute also operates the popular online resource CatholicExchange.com. *Catholic Exchange* provides world news from a Catholic perspective as well as daily devotionals and articles that will help readers to grow in holiness and live a life consistent with the teachings of the Church.

In 2013, Sophia Institute launched Sophia Institute for Teachers to renew and rebuild Catholic culture through service to Catholic education. With the goal of nurturing the spiritual, moral, and cultural life of souls, and an abiding respect for the role and work of teachers, we strive to provide materials and programs that are at once enlightening to the mind and ennobling to the heart; faithful and complete, as well as useful and practical.

Sophia Institute gratefully recognizes the Solidarity Association for preserving and encouraging the growth of our apostolate over the course of many years. Without their generous and timely support, this book would not be in your hands.

www.SophiaInstitute.com
www.CatholicExchange.com
www.SophiaInstituteforTeachers.org

Sophia Institute Press is a registered trademark of Sophia Institute.
Sophia Institute is a tax-exempt institution as defined by the
Internal Revenue Code, Section 501(c)(3). Tax ID 22-2548708.